50 hikes

in the
White Mountains

OTHER BOOKS BY DANIEL DOAN

The Crystal Years
Amos Jackman
50 More Hikes in New Hampshire
Dan Doan's Fitness Program for Hikers and Cross-Country Skiers
Our Last Backpack
Indian Stream Republic: Settling a New England Frontier, 1785–1842

OTHER BOOKS BY RUTH DOAN MACDOUGALL

The Lilting House
The Cost of Living
One Minus One
The Cheerleader
Wife and Mother
Aunt Pleasantine
The Flowers of the Forest
A Lovely Time Was Had by All
Snowy

50 *hikes*
in the
White Mountains

Hikes and Backpacking Trips in the
High Peaks Region of New Hampshire

Fifth Edition

DANIEL DOAN
AND RUTH DOAN MACDOUGALL

Backcountry Publications
Woodstock, Vermont

An Invitation to the Reader
Developments, logging, and fires all take their toll on hiking trails, often from one year to the next. If you find that conditions along these 50 hikes have changed, please let the publisher know, so that corrections can be made in future editions. Address all correspondence to:

Editor, 50 Hikes™
Backcountry Guides
PO Box 748
Woodstock, VT 05091

Library of Congress Cataloging-in-Publication Data
Doan, Daniel.
   50 hikes in the White Mountains : hikes and backpacking trips in the High Peaks region of New Hampshire / Daniel Doan and Ruth Doan MacDougall. — 5th ed.
      p.   cm.
   Rev. ed. of: Fifty hikes in the White Mountains. 4th ed. ©1990.
   Includes index.
   ISBN 0-88150-389-4 (alk. paper)
   1. Hiking—White Mountains (N.H. and Me.)—Guidebooks. 2. Backpacking—White Mountains (N.H. and Me.)—Guidebooks. 3. White Mountains (N.H. and Me.)—Guidebooks. 4. New Hampshire—Guidebooks. I. MacDougall, Ruth Doan, 1939–. II. Doan, Daniel, 1914–1993. Fifty hikes in the White Mountains. III. Title. IV. Series: Fifty hikes series.
   GV199.42.W47D63   1997
   917.42'2—dc21
                                                            96-48312
                                                                CIP

Published by Backcountry Guides
A division of The Countryman Press
PO Box 748
Woodstock, Vermont 05091

Distributed by W.W. Norton & Company, Inc.
500 Fifth Avenue
New York, NY 10110

Series design by Glenn Suokko
Page composition by Molly Cook Field
Trail overlays by Richard Widhu
Cover photograph of Franconia Ridge from Mount Lafayette by Robert J. Kozlow
Photograph on page 31 by Fred Bavendam. Photographs on pages 98, 113, and 139 by Robert J. Kozlow. Photographs on pages 120 and 134 by Ruth Doan MacDougall.

Printed in the United States of America
10 9 8 7 6 5 4 3

Acknowledgments

Thanks to all who have helped keep these hikes updated, especially the following:

Donald K. MacDougall
Marjorie M. Doan
Christopher Lloyd
Mary L. Kibling
Steven D. Smith
Hal and Peggy Graham of Trailwrights
Kirk Dougal
Amy Gumprecht
The Over the Hill Hikers of Sandwich, NH
The Appalachian Mountain Club and the US Forest Service

Trying to analyze what he did when he went through the woods, he discovered that there were many little tricks to make it easier. He'd never thought about it before. You didn't watch your feet, but looked beyond and remembered the branches and rocks in the way. You timed your pace until you knew almost without glancing down what was in front of you while your eyes moved on ahead. You kept in mind the sun, when it showed through the clouds, and the sound of the brook. You used your hands to fend aside the branches and you balanced easy on your feet to suit the roughness of the ground and twisted your shoulders to slip around the trees.

—Daniel Doan
Amos Jackman

50 Hikes at a Glance

	Distance (in miles)	Rise (in feet)	Views	Good for kids	Waterfalls	Notes
1. Sabbaday Falls	1	100	✓	✓		Simple & lovely
2. West Rattlesnake Mountain	2	460	✓	✓		Lakes Region view
3. Boulder Loop	3.25	900	✓	✓		Keyed to educational stops
4. Kedron Flume	2	600	✓	✓	✓	Rugged mountain fastness
5. Three Ponds	5.5	500		✓	✓	Fine for gaining woods experience
6. East Pond	3	780		✓		Can include Little East Pond
7. Greeley Ponds	4	400		✓		Perfect for picnics
8. Old Mast Road & Kelley Trail	5	1000		✓	✓	Woods walk & rock scramble
9. Belknap Mountain	1.5	740	✓	✓		Blueberries!
10. Plymouth Mountain	3	894	✓	✓		Little known & unspoiled
11. Mount Major	3	1000	✓	✓		Stone hut ruins on summit
12. Hedgehog Mountain	5	1300	✓	✓		Vistas from ledges
13. Stinson Mountain	3.5	1390	✓	✓		Especially fine in October
14. Mount Cardigan	3.5	1220	✓	✓		Distinctive rock dome
15. Smarts Mountain	6	1938	✓	✓		The Daniel Doan Trail
16. Artist Bluff & Bald Mountain	1.5	400	✓	✓		Get a hiker's perspective
17. Mount Pemigewasset	3.5	1170	✓	✓		The Indian Head
18. Basin–Cascades Trail	2.3	500		✓	✓	Woods, falls, rock formations
19. Lonesome Lake	3.25	1000	✓	✓		Mtn. lake in spectacular setting
20. Mount Flume	10	3367	✓		✓	Rock slides & exposed ledges
21. Mount Liberty	8	3100	✓			Stepped rock summit
22. Mount Lincoln	8	3350	✓		✓	Can include Mount Lafayette
23. Mount Lafayette	7.75	3500	✓			Highest peak in Franconia Range
24. North Lafayette	9	3360	✓			Remote from the crowd
25. Cannon Mountain	7.5	2100	✓	?		Hiking alternative to tramway

	Distance (in miles)	Rise (in feet)	Views	Good for kids	Waterfalls	Notes
Franconia Notch Region						
26. Mount Kinsman	10	3400	✓			Two summits
27. Mount Moosilauke	6.75	2400	✓	?		"Dartmouth's Mountain"
28. Mount Garfield	9.5	3100	✓	?		Logging history
29. Mount Osceola	6.5	2025	✓			Highest of Waterville Valley mtns.
30. Mount Tripyramid	11	3035	✓			Three peaks & two slides!
31. Between the Notches: Zeacliff	7.5	1500	✓	✓	✓	Pemigewasset Wilderness views
Mount Washington Region						
32. Pinkham Notch: Crew-Cut Tr.	1.75	400	✓	✓		Introduction to Pinkham
33. Lowe's Bald Spot	4.25	1000	✓	✓		Experience Mt. Washington
34. Glen Boulder	3	1800	✓	?	✓	A landmark
35. Tuckerman Ravine	6.5	2300	✓	?	✓	To the Snow Arch
36. Mount Washington	9	3675	✓		✓	The western approach
37. The Alpine Garden	8.5	3500	✓			Flowers: mid-June to July
38. Mount Jefferson	5	2700	✓			Memorable ledges: the Caps
39. Mount Adams	9	4500	✓			2nd in height to Mt. Washington
40. Mount Madison	10.5	3800	✓		✓	End of Presidential Range
41. Mount Kearsarge North	6	2600	✓	?		NH & Maine views
42. Tom-Field-Avalon Loop	8	2800	✓		✓	Three summits
43. Mt. Starr King/Mt. Waumbeck	7.5	2600	✓	?		See the Presidentials from the north
44. Mount Eisenhower	6.5	2725	✓	?		Great trail construction
45. Mount Crawford	5	2100	✓	✓		Historic & rewarding hike
Backpacking Hikes						
46. Mount Hancock	9.5	2400	✓	✓		Test yourself gently
47. Sandwich Mountain	13	2500	✓	✓		Camp at Black Mt. Pond
48. East Branch/Mount Carrigain	28	3300	✓		✓	Pemigewasset Wilderness
49. Mount Isolation	14	3200	✓			A remote peak
50. Mahoosuc Range	33	8600	✓		✓	A weeklong adventure

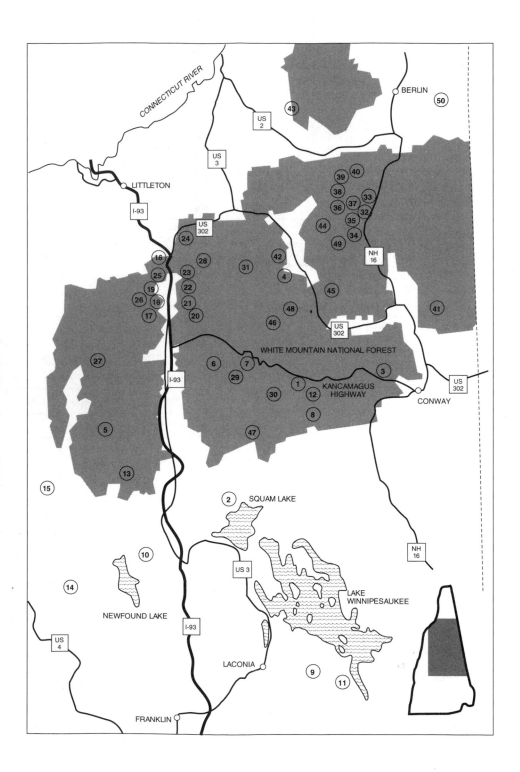

Contents

MOUNT WASHINGTON REGION

BACKPACKING HIKES

Preface to the Fifth Edition

The first mountain I ever climbed with Dan, my father, was Belknap Mountain near our home in Laconia, and according to family legend I didn't make it to the summit on foot. Dan carried me, while on his back in his wicker pack basket he lugged my baby sister, Penny.

My mother, Ernie, who was definitely not the outdoors type, found this awfully funny, and Dan was always amused by the recollection. I don't remember that hike at all, but in the ensuing years Belknap became an auxiliary backyard where we picked bushels of blueberries and I learned the heady rewards of the views from the tower.

Backpacking was called "camping out" in my childhood. An overnight trip to Sawyer River provided my earliest and most enduring memory of camping out: stretches of clear water over golden rocks and pebbles. This is one of those indelible, beautiful images that are lifelong treasures.

Dan's hiking and camping equipment had various histories, usually dating back to his boyhood. Penny and I eventually added our Girl Scout mess kits to the collection of blackened pots. Dissatisfied with his tent, Dan designed one that Ernie sewed, a major project. There were assorted old fishing rods, including at least one bamboo pole, but Penny and I were outfitted with new smaller ones; we fished with him in ponds and brooks and lakes. I grew up thinking that the smell of trout frying over a campfire, of balsam and spruce boughs crushed under a sleeping bag, and an overall aroma of fly dope were the essence of life.

I was tantalized by the lure of cities, but since Dan had chosen the country instead, I knew in my bones that he had given me the foundation on which to base my wanderings. The love of nature was second nature to Penny and me, because of Dan.

Another legacy he gave me was the love of writing. Throughout my childhood I fell asleep listening to what I would later call a literary lullaby, the sound of Dan's typewriter as he wrote at night after work. By the time I was six, I had resolved that I too would be a writer.

I did leave New Hampshire. My husband, Don, and I lived in Massachusetts and England, but our inclinations tugged us back to our home state. When we finally settled in Center Sandwich, our choice of towns was decided by its proximity to the White Mountain National Forest.

So I've returned to that foundation Dan gave me. And I am a writer, mostly of novels. My stepmother, Marjorie (whom Dan married after Ernie died and who *is* the outdoors type), once asked Dan, "What kind of writer is Ruthie?" He replied, "An impressionist." A high compliment.

He had helped me with my work; there came a time when I could help with his.

Diabetes and a stroke brought an end to his hiking but not to his writing. He began a memoir, *Our Last Backpack*. His typing, self-taught, had always been full of rebellious keys, and it was more so after the stroke. In the past, I had typed some final drafts of manuscripts for him, but now as he wrote his memoir I typed the manuscript through its drafts and edited it. I was so happy to be able to do this; I think it gave me a feeling of control over my distress about the tragic irony of Dan's fate: a strong, athletic man, a hiker, gradually losing the use of his legs. His physical therapist told me, "He's a fighter." Dan fought hard in the diminishing stages from cane to wheelchair to bed, and I think the work on *Our Last Backpack* gave him too a sense of control.

During this time I discussed with him what to do about his hiking books. Ever since they were first published, he had been flabbergasted and delighted by their success, amazed as their popularity continued and they became classics. He felt a great responsibility to keep them updated. I wanted to shoulder this responsibility, but there was one problem. I was just emerging from a 10-year spell of agoraphobia that had made me almost housebound. Could I climb mountains again?

The challenge galvanized me. Once more I was hiking. And because I carried Dan's hiking books, making notes as I checked the trails, I was still hiking with him. He supervised the trail changes I wrote for new printings. When he died in September 1993, he knew that his hiking books would be living on.

This new edition of *50 Hikes in the White Mountains* has three new hikes in it. Over the years a few of the introductory hikes had become no longer suited to Dan's original purposes, so I have substituted West Rattlesnake Mountain, Hedgehog Mountain, and Smarts Mountain.

To Dan's thoughts in his Introduction I would only add some equipment suggestions for day hikes. No doubt you will develop your own list of essentials. Besides the items Dan mentions in the "Clothing and Equipment" section, my day hikes list includes an extra pair of socks, a bandanna, sunscreen, and a flashlight. I also carry more than the quart of water he suggests. No matter how short the hike, I bring along 2 quarts; they increase the weight of my pack but also increase my feeling of security.

As Dan used to sign his books: Happy hiking!

—*Ruth Doan MacDougall*
Winter 1997

Introduction

These excursions into New Hampshire's White Mountains are intended to initiate the beginner and entertain the experienced hiker. There are 45 day hikes and 5 overnight backpacking hikes. They are arranged from short to long and from gradual to steep. The first 4 hikes are suitable for family outings. Then there are 4 woods walks, 7 hikes in small mountains, and 30 hikes in and around the Franconia Range and the Presidential Range. The five backpacking hikes run from a weekend to a week. Some of the hikes loop around to their starting points, which are, of course, the places where you leave your car. Other hikes follow the same route up to their destinations and back.

Most of the hikes are within the central White Mountains. There are several that take you to lesser-known outlying summits. The corners of the hiking territory are: Mount Major (Hike 11), southeast near Lake Winnipesaukee; Mount Cardigan (Hike 14), southwest near Canaan; Mount Starr King (Hike 43), northwest in Jefferson; and Old Speck Mountain (Hike 50), northeast at Grafton Notch, Maine. Within this area, the hikes take you up all the major peaks of the White Mountains. The map facing the contents page shows clearly the location of each hike.

The White Mountain hiking season extends from May into October. Winter weather occurs early and late. Above treeline, you may encounter icy storms at any time, even during the season. June and July have their blackflies and mosquitoes; you'll need insect repellent. To my mind, September is the best hiking month. The heat of July, the August haze, and the bugs are gone for the season. Cool air and clear skies offset the customary September storms.

THE TRAILS

The hikes follow established, well-marked trails maintained by the US Forest Service, the New Hampshire Division of Parks, the Appalachian Mountain Club (AMC), and various other clubs. Forty-five of the hikes are in the White Mountain National Forest or in nearby state reservations. Some of the hikes begin on, or cross, land owned by lumber companies, by Dartmouth College, or other private property. On trails crossing bound-

Mount Washington

aries between private land and the national forest, the forest service posts small yellow signs at the boundaries. Any abuse of the privilege granted to hikers on this private land could result in NO TRESPASSING signs.

The mountain trails change due to slides, washouts, new beaver ponds, trees downed by winds, and heavy use. On the other hand, some, like the Crawford Path, have hardly changed in more than 100 years. When necessary, trails, or sections of them, are relocated. Access roads and parking places may be restricted or relocated. For latest information, check with the US Forest Service, the Appalachian Mountain Club, or the New Hampshire Department of Resources and Economic Development.

The composite maps, featuring topographic base maps with the de-scribed hiking route superimposed on them, allow the hiker to appraise the terrain and to gauge hiking difficulty and distance. These maps use portions of both United States Geological Survey (USGS) and Forest Service (USDA) quadrangles. The latter are of more recent vintage and are therefore more up-to-date in terms of trails, roads, and other man-made features. Both use the USGS contour base. Road and trail numbers on the forest service quads are for administrative purposes and are of no particular consequence to hikers. The USGS maps are available in a variety of retail outlets, especially sporting goods stores, as well as directly from the federal government. The forest service maps can be purchased at the White Mountain National Forest headquarters in Laconia or at their five district ranger stations. Any serious hiker should also equip himself with the *AMC White Mountain Guide* and the excellent maps that come along with it. The AMC maps are kept as modern as possible by reissues with each edition of the *Guide*. The most accurate map of all for a portion of the White Mountains is Brad Washburn's "Mount Washington and the Heart of the Presidential Range," also published by the AMC. The *AMC White Mountain Guide* and Washburn's Mount Washington map may be purchased at Pinkham Notch Visitor Center and at sporting goods stores, outfitters, and bookstores throughout New Hampshire.

LOGGING ROADS

The descriptions of the hikes refer often to logging roads. Almost all of these are *old* logging roads and have become part of the new forests. They are not raw bulldozed cuts for heavy modern logging machines. Only the trails keep them open. The old roads were graded for horses and sleds; although plentifully strewn with rocks, they follow the slopes at gentle angles. Together with the former railroad grades along the valleys, these old logging roads provide the best walking in the mountains.

The present logging operations supervised by the forest service usually leave the trails in wooded corridors. When you look off from various summits, you will see the clear-cuts as irregular squares or rectangles of slash or sprouts. Many new access roads lead to these clear-cuts, and such roads are often gated.

The Pemigewasset Wilderness, whose mountains and rivers are drained by the East Branch of the Pemigewasset River, is a fascinating former logging territory, and a splendid example of new forests on land once devastated by logging and fires. Now officially a wilderness, it contains a network of trails connecting with the main Wilderness Trail, which in turn connects with the Kancamagus Highway by way of the Lincoln Woods Trail.

DISTANCE, WALKING TIME, AND VERTICAL RISE

Each hike description begins with the figures for distance, walking time, and vertical rise. These are gauges by which you can evaluate the hikes.

The times allow for leisurely climbing, which seems to me the only pleasant and sensible way, but they do not include rest periods, lunch breaks, view gazing, or bird watching. Young, hardy climbers may cut the times in half.

The vertical-rise figure tells you the approximate distance up. If you start at a 1000-foot elevation and climb to a 2500-foot summit, you may walk 2 miles or 5, but your vertical rise is 1500 feet. Sometimes you climb down into a valley and up again to a summit; your return trip will thus include some climbing, which is included in the total, or round-trip, vertical rise figure. As a general rule, you can expect that the greater the vertical rise per mile, the more strenuous the climb.

THE WHITE MOUNTAIN NATIONAL FOREST

The State of New Hampshire had disposed of its public land by the mid-1800s, and logging began in earnest after the Civil War. Men with axes felled trees throughout the north country—except in the White Mountains' most remote valleys, where the steep slopes presented transportation problems. The rivers were too shallow and rocky for log drives.

Because of this and other difficulties, the forests of red spruce, pine, hemlock, and cedar in the White Mountains remained standing until late in the era, and some were bypassed completely as lumbermen cut a swath from Maine to Minnesota.

Finally, railroads opened the valleys in the 1880s and 1890s, and much of the timber was cut by 1900. Logging continued through the First World War and even as late as the 1930s, but, long before the cutting was complete, forest fires had devastated large tracts of cut-over land.

Conservationists, led primarily by the Society for the Protection of New Hampshire Forests, came to the rescue of the White Mountains in the early 1900s. The federal government purchased areas for watershed protection under the Weeks Act beginning in 1912. The White Mountain National Forest now covers over 770,000 acres, a portion of which extends into Maine.

The land is managed by the US Forest Service under directives based on "multiple use." Among these uses are timber production, watershed protection, recreation development, and wildlife protection. Ten Scenic Areas have been designated by the forest service. In addition, there are five Wilderness Areas mandated by Congress: Great Gulf, Presidential–Dry River (both on Mount Washington), Pemigewasset, Sandwich Range, and Caribou-Speckled. The five Wilderness Areas preserve a total of 114,932 acres of valleys, ponds, and mountains in their natural beauty.

Ruth's Note: In 1997 the White Mountain National Forest began participating in a "user-fee program." Parking passes are now required where signs designate fee areas. These passports can be purchased at the White Mountain National Forest headquarters in Laconia, at ranger stations, and at local businesses. For more information, phone the Androscoggin Ranger station at (603)466-2713, extension 213.

TREES AND ANIMALS

The mountainsides are now covered by hardwood forests of beech, maple, yellow birch, and white birch, which took over after the destruction of the spruce. Evergreens remain predominant in the swamps. The upper summits, from about 3000 feet to treeline, are spruce/fir forests interspersed with white birch and mountain ash.

You will probably meet no dangerous animal life. This is not rattlesnake country. Black bears and wildcats are shy. I recall only six bears in 55 years of walking the mountains, and they were all going away fast when they became aware of me. However, black bears can be a problem at campsites, so take careful precautions not to attract them. Do your cooking at least 100 feet downwind of the campsite, and keep your food and cooking utensils separate from your sleeping area. Put food scraps in closed containers. Hang the food at least 10 feet off the ground and 5 feet out on a limb that won't support a bear.

Porcupines can be dangerous to an aggressive dog; otherwise they mind their own business. Even *Homo sapiens* seems gentler in the mountains.

White-tailed deer are forest denizens seldom seen in the higher mountains. You probably won't see one of the eastern coyotes now roaming the region; they survive by avoiding men, and have been doing so successfully since their arrival in the 1970s. You may see a moose. They have become more common; you'll certainly see their ox-like tracks. Fishers, otters, mink, and weasels are not often seen.

flash quickly into cover. Red squirrels and chipmunks will chatter at you. Coons, skunks, foxes, and flying squirrels come out at night.

In the text I mention birds because I like to watch them. (Ravens are common now but were not when I described the hikes first in 1972.) Trees, flowers, and plants mean more if you know their names. Field books to identify these, the birds, and the animals, will increase your enjoyment.

CLOTHING AND EQUIPMENT

Careful consideration and selection of the clothing and equipment for your hikes are essential. Basic apparel includes a cotton-polyester blend shirt, walking pants or shorts, comfortable underwear, and hiking shoes worn over two pairs of socks.

You should consider the modern lightweight hiking boots. They are based on designs and materials from jogging shoes. During a long hike in these boots you can avoid lifting a ton or more of the boot-weight required if you had worn a pair of clumpers. I wear canvas and leather with a relatively thin lug sole, about 2 pounds— but not for backpacking. And even for hiking, if your feet aren't accustomed to mountain trails, you need the protection of a more conventional leather boot. Break in your boots completely before you commit your feet to a long hike in them. This applies to both standard leather boots and the lightweights. Heavy mountaineering boots are unnecessary for the hikes in this book.

As for socks, one pair of light wool socks under one pair of heavy wool socks seems to be the best combination. Hikers favor the ragg-knit type.

Pants should be loose.

As long as the weather is fair, the above clothing is all you'll need to wear. Pack the rest of your equipment and spare clothes in a strong, waterproof knapsack, usually called a "day pack." Don't dangle equipment from belt or shoulder straps. No bulging pockets. Here's what you'll need: heavy wool shirt, sweater, or insulated jacket; poncho or rain suit with hood; nylon parka or shell; hat; gloves; warm pants; matches and firestarter in a waterproof container; compass; map and guidebook; pocketknife with can opener and screwdriver; a quart of water in a canteen or other container; lunch; and spare food for two meals.

Consider buying a parka made of one of the laminated materials that are microporous, making them both breathable and waterproof. There are many such parkas in a wide range of styles and uses. The materials are also used for rain pants and the uppers of boots. Though expensive, this type of clothing can eliminate your other rain gear for active, sweat-inducing exercise, but don't expect a miracle of total sweat evaporation. Such a parka can be substituted at times for a windproof shell.

Down-filled jackets are comfortable beyond dreams as long as they're dry, but when they're wet I wish I had on that warm-though-wet product, wool.

If you're backpacking, you'll need everything on the day hiker's list and more. In addition to an adequately large pack (too varied for discussion here), you'll want to take a tent, or at least a waterproof tarp; a hiker's gasoline or cartridge-type gas stove, cook kit, forks and spoons; a sleeping bag in a stuff sack; a foam pad to place under your sleeping bag at night; a small first aid kit, including moleskin for foot blisters (no snakebite kit necessary, but take insect repellent); soap and a towel; a small flashlight, two candles, and extra matches in a waterproof container; a

AMC Hutman on Mount Lafayette

I like a plastic transparent compass with movable base for setting a course. (Note: In the White Mountains your compass points about 16 degrees west.) I also use plastic flask-shaped water bottles (1-pint size) instead of a canteen.

Because equipment for backpacking is so extensive, and the choice arouses such vehement contention, you may want to read a book on the subject and explore a shop or catalog that specializes in backpacking and mountaineering equipment. If you are new to backpacking, I suggest you rent your pack, tent, and other gear for the first few trips to learn what you will want to buy. Whatever you finally decide to take, be sure to set everything up at home and try it out before heading into the mountains.

RULES AND REGULATIONS

All rules and guidelines for hikers in the White Mountains, both those of the forest service and those promoted by the Appalachian Mountain Club, have been developed to save the forest from its greatest enemy, fire, and to preserve the areas that are becoming more and more popular, especially those with delicate ecology near treeline and above in the alpine zone. The days of the roaring campfire and the woodsman's bough bed are over.

The rules apply mostly to campers and backpackers, rather than to day hikers. Common sense and thoughtful consideration of others will go far to direct your behavior into conformation with rules, but there are some regulations you should know about. Hikers on private property cannot legally build wood or charcoal fires without the landowner's permission and a fire permit from the district fire chief. Use a portable stove. No overnight camping is allowed on private

small hatchet or saw (optional); 50 feet of light nylon cord for a variety of uses, including hanging food from trees out of reach of bears; and meals for each day of the trip. Food should be light and easy to prepare. Include ready-to-eat food for lunches. Standard necessities can be found at your supermarket: oatmeal, sugar, dried milk, tea, salt, hard-breads, cheese, canned meats, dried soups, etc. At your backpacking shop choose freeze-dried foods for super-light nourishment.

Equipment is no substitute for experience. Learning how to walk in the woods is more important than the best hiking boots money can buy.

property without the landowner's permission. Carry out all your trash. Don't cut trees or boughs or destroy plants. Park your car well off roads. Don't park in any opening into the woods no matter how ancient, and of course never in any logging road or in front of a gate. A state law prohibits obstruction of a right-of-way.

For the White Mountain National Forest the long-standing requirement of fire permits was discontinued in 1985. There are, however, special regulations about camping and fires. You should get the latest seasonal information from the office of the forest supervisor in Laconia, or from visitor centers at the district ranger stations in Conway, Gorham, and Bethlehem. The forest service also maintains a visitor center at Lincoln Woods on the western end of the Kancamagus Highway, and a visitor center in Bethel, Maine.

The AMC offers information at Pinkham Notch Visitor Center, at Lafayette Place in Franconia Notch, and at the former depot near the Crawford House site.

The State of New Hampshire has rules for its parks, reservations, and forests. In general no camping or wood or charcoal fires are allowed outside designated campgrounds and picnic areas. Regulations are posted. The NH Division of Parks and Recreation provides a brochure, "NH Camping Guide."

Although in the White Mountain National Forest fire permits are no longer required, you must obtain and abide by the forest service publication "Backcountry Camping Rules," which provides detailed listings of current limitations on camping and fires. Where overuse has compacted the soil and damaged plants and trees, natural recovery is encouraged by

Forest Protection Areas (formerly called Restricted Use Areas, or RUAs) and future harm is prevented. Furthermore, no camping is allowed above treeline, which has been set at the altitude where trees are less than 8 feet high. Similar restrictions—no camping, no wood or charcoal fires—are in effect on land 200 feet from many trails, and within 0.25 mile around various huts, shelters, tent platforms, and lakes. (Two hundred feet is hardly enough distance to stay away from *any* trails when pitching your tent, at least to my mind.) Certain roadsides have 0.25-mile protection. On trails in the national forest you'll be alerted by signs posted at Forest Protection Area boundaries. The forest service offers helpful brochures on recreational uses of the national forest.

Camping permits are not required in the Wilderness Areas. Campsite use is limited to 10 persons at one time. Check the latest regulations when you get your "Backcountry Camping Rules."

I cannot emphasize enough your obligation to stay on trails when you are above treeline. Fragile alpine plants are at the mercy of hiking boots and once damaged may never recover. The mountains and your fellow hikers deserve an uncluttered trail. No litter, no trash left behind. And no random elimination—to put it politely, copy the cat, and make sure you're 100 long paces away from any trail, stream, pond, or spring. No candy wrappers, no cans or aluminum envelopes or any of the slick packages our civilization provides us for throwing away. If you take them in, take them out again in your pack. The motto is: "Carry in and carry out!" And another: "Leave only your footprints."

HUTS AND SHELTERS

In the White Mountains the Appalachian Mountain Club and the forest service maintain most of the trails and shelters. Open-front shelters of logs or boards face stone fireplaces. The Appalachian Mountain Club has built closed huts or lodges to serve hikers on its trail system.

Long a prime mover in this area, the AMC was founded in 1876. It maintains over 1200 miles of trails, including 350 miles of the Appalachian Trail, as well as shelters and mountain huts. In the huts, crews of college students provide meals and lodging for hikers during July and August; some of the huts are open from the middle of June into October. Winter accommodations (carry your own food and equipment) are available at two huts having caretakers. Inquire at Pinkham Notch Visitor Center for reservations and rates. This center for AMC activities in the White Mountains on NH 16 is open year-round to accommodate skiers and hikers, and it also serves as headquarters for the system of trails, shelters, and huts.

A note on winter excursions: Snowshoes and cross-country skis can extend your season to almost 12 months. Both sports are fascinating but require learning and experience for full enjoyment and safety.

PHYSICAL FITNESS

Good physical condition increases hiking pleasure. Without it, the more strenuous hikes are no pleasure at all, and there may be harm and danger.

If you wait until warm weather to get in shape, the arrangement of hikes in this book will break the news to your body that you're going to take it walking. Nobody has to be an athlete to succeed with Hike 1; Mount Washington is something else again. In preparation for the longer climbs in the high Franconias and Presidentials, I've included a few relatively easy hikes for each region. In the Franconia Region, they are numbers 16, 17, 18, and 19. In the Presidentials, they are numbers 32, 33, 34, and 35.

Stamina developed for walking and climbing provides not only pleasure but an important safety margin in the mountains. It's a form of insurance you can take out yourself.

SAFETY

Almost every year, the mountains claim some hiker's life. Storms are sudden and fierce above treeline. Trails over the bare rocks, marked only by cairns and signs at the junctions, disappear in the clouds and wind-driven rain, sleet, and snow. Electrical storms shoot down lightning that bounces from the rocks amid the torrential rain. Besides physical fitness, two precautions may help you survive these dangers. First, in the face of threatening weather forecasts, don't go mountain climbing, or go to some lesser peak or a woods trail. Second, in the face of gathering low clouds and wind at treeline, turn back. The woods and shelter are only a few steps behind you; ahead you will climb into increasingly thick fog and winds so strong you'll be unable to stand.

On many trails leading above treeline, a forest service sign will warn you of the dangers ahead. They aren't kidding, either; above treeline you're in hazardous territory. Perhaps this fact, along with the tremendous views and the thrill of being there on your own two feet, gives above-treeline hiking its excitement.

It's important to hike with a companion. (Two old friends hike best together; I've been lucky this way.) Stay together. This is a rule of every mountain clubber, experienced climber, and all officials delegated to find the lost or injured lone hiker.

Carry a compass. Carry a map that you have studied so you know about the route and the trails. Be prepared to spend a night out in the woods or under a rock. This means carrying extra food, water, warm clothing, and waterproof outerwear in a knapsack.

Purity of drinking water cannot be assumed just because a stream is clear and cold and tumbling down a sylvan valley. It might contain *Giardia lamblia,* a common intestinal parasite, which causes delayed diarrhea, cramps, loss of appetite and weight, as well as other unpleasant symptoms. Among animals other than humans, beavers are likely to infect streams and ponds in the mountains. Boiling, filtration, and chemical treatment are now standard preventive measures. The forest service offers an information sheet titled "Is the Water Safe?" Note that my mention of water in these hikes does not mean safe water.

And last of all—but so important it might be first—before you set out, tell someone where you're going, and give an alternate place for bad weather. Then go there, one or the other, and enjoy yourself. The hike is supposed to be fun. No bitching: not about the trail, the weather, or the world. Leave that attitude back with "civilization" and your other troubles.

I wish you years and years of great hikes in the White Mountains of New Hampshire.

ADDRESSES

Appalachian Mountain Club
5 Joy Street
Boston, Massachusetts 02108
or
Pinkham Notch Visitor Center
Gorham, New Hampshire 03581

White Mountain National Forest
Supervisor's Office
719 Main Street
Laconia, New Hampshire 03246

**New Hampshire Department
of Resources and Economic
Development**
Concord, New Hampshire 03301

**Society for the Protection of New
Hampshire Forests**
54 Portsmouth Street
Concord, New Hampshire 03301

United States Geological Survey
Box 25286, Denver Federal Center
Denver, Colorado 80225

KEY TO MAP SYMBOLS

— — — main trail

• • • side trail

Appalachian Trail

shelter

ⓟ parking

INTRODUCTORY HIKES

His senses seemed to expand and reach out toward the woods and hills around him, absorbing the pine smell, the green trees and blue sky, the soft earth, the muted bird calls and the breeze in the boughs. His senses focused all these things like a magnifying glass concentrating the sun's rays until he was on fire with joy.

—Daniel Doan
The Crystal Years

1

Sabbaday Falls

Distance (picnic area to falls and back): 1 mile

Walking time: ½ hour

Vertical rise: 100 feet

Maps: USDA/FS 7½' Mt. Tripyramid; USGS 15' Mt. Chocorua

No more than an afternoon's jaunt, this popular short hike to Sabbaday Falls conveys an important message about the mountains. It suggests a new world to explore: one filled with outdoor sights, sounds, and sensations. It arouses a new or forgotten interest in the woods, the streams, and the miles of mountainous terrain around you.

How to Get There
The Sabbaday Brook Trail begins 16 miles west of Conway and NH 16 at a picnic area on the south side of the Kancamagus Highway. The graded path in a forest of maple, beech, and birch leads up to the base of the ledges through which the stream cuts its way.

The Trail
At the Sabbaday Falls sign, turn left down to the lower pool. Stone steps and peeled-log railings ease the way up the ledges above the narrow flume that was formed by water wearing away

Upper Sabbaday Falls

FRED BAVENDAM

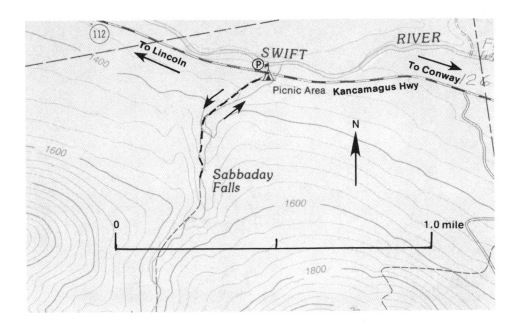

a basalt dike in surrounding granite. From a deep pothole, the stream pours down into the flume. The walkway returns to the Sabbaday Brook Trail above the falls. (The Sabbaday Brook Trail continues up the brook toward Mount Tripyramid.) Take the trail back to your car.

Westward, the Kancamagus Highway rises steadily to Kancamagus Pass at 2855 feet, then winds down to Lincoln and I-93 at North Woodstock, about 20 miles away. Signs mark other trails into the mountains north and south. (See hikes to Greeley Ponds, number 7, and Mount Hancock, number 46.) Before driving the highway, check your car's gas gauge; there are no service stations on the 34 miles between Conway and Lincoln, and across the central 15 miles, no buildings.

The adventure of driving the highway persists despite its accepted use and blacktop surface added in 1963. Before that, many tourists did not know of the completion of the gravel road's upper section, done in the summer of 1959, and uncertainty added spice. One tourist stopped near the Conway end to question an old lady rocking on her porch: "Does this road go across the mountains?" After a moment's thought she told him: "Well, a lot of cars pass by here and don't come back."

2

West Rattlesnake Mountain

Distance (round trip): 2 miles	

Walking time: 1 hour

Vertical rise: 460 feet

Maps: USDA/FS 7½' Squam Mountains; USGS 7½' Squam Mountains

This hike delivers a lot of bang for the buck. A gentle, easy climb leads you to one of the most beautiful views in the Lakes Region.

At the summit of this 1260-foot western peak of the Rattlesnakes, you look down on Squam Lake, its blue emphasized by the many green islands and the green shoreline curving around coves and inlets. The boats down there are as tiny as water bugs, scooting along leaving silent wakes.

In the distance you see more water, Lake Winnipesaukee, and mountains. Red Hill is nearest on the southeast, then Copple Crown, Belknap Mountain, Piper Mountain, and Mount Major, with Mount Kearsarge and Ragged

Mountain to the southwest and Bridgewater Mountain and Hersey Mountain on the west.

How to Get There

If you're coming from the south, turn off US 3 in Holderness onto NH 113. After 5 miles you'll notice on the right a sign indicating a road to Rockywold and Deephaven camps. Continue on NH 113 about 0.5 mile farther to a parking area on the left. This also serves as parking for the Mount Morgan Trail. (See Hike 20 in *50 More Hikes in New Hampshire*.)

From the north on NH 113, drive from the overhead yellow light in Center Sandwich 6.3 miles to the parking area, on the right.

The Trail

Turn right and walk along the highway about 100 yards. The Old Bridle Path trailhead is on your left, just before a private driveway to a house. There is a signboard a few steps into the woods: WEST RATTLESNAKE, A NATURAL AREA OF THE UNIVERSITY OF NEW HAMPSHIRE FOR EDUCATION AND RESEARCH. There may be flyers provided by the Squam Lakes Association, explaining that fires, camping, and all vehicles

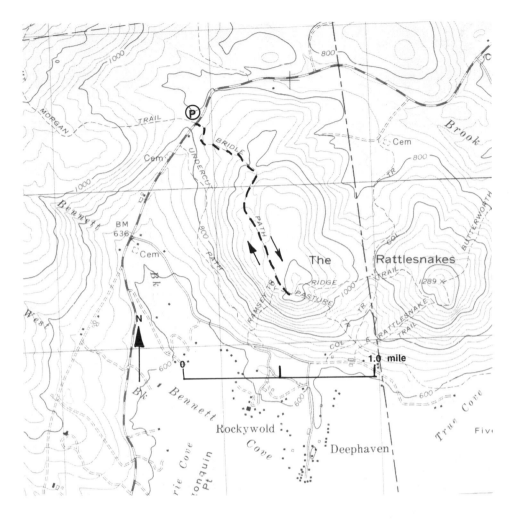

are prohibited in these 70 acres owned
by UNH.

The Old Bridle Path is a wide, leafy
trail, with rocks and roots to make
you keep an eye on your footing. You
climb rock steps and log stairs. Stone
walls in the woods show that this land
was once farmed. You may hear a
hawk's piercing call. You pass blueberry bushes and perhaps glimpse a
chipmunk.

At a ledge near the top, a small
wooded arrow points left toward the
summit. Ignore the unmarked trail

directly ahead; it's an alternate route
to the Ramsey Trail.

On the summit, you see Squam
Lakes Association markers for the
various trails from East Rattlesnake
and a sign for the Armstrong Natural
Area. But mostly you see the famous
view.

Corral your kids. These ledges have
dangerous drops, so everybody should
stay well back from the edge.

As you descend the Old Bridle Path,
you'll be thinking about exploring the
Rattlesnakes some more another day.

3

Boulder Loop

Distance (around the loop, including spur to ledges): 3¼ miles

Walking time: 3 hours

Vertical rise: 900 feet

Maps: USDA/FS 7½' North Conway West; USGS 15' North Conway

The Boulder Loop Trail is for family walking and enjoyment. It is keyed to stops described in the forest service pamphlet available at the Passaconaway Historic Site or at the Saco District Ranger Station in Conway at the corner of NH 16 and the Kancamagus Highway.

The trail should be considered a climb rather than a picnic jaunt. Suitable shoes and other clothing are necessary. A small knapsack frees your hands of lunch, camera, and jacket. Remember to use the pack for carrying out your empty soft-drink bottles and cans and cellophane wrappers.

How to Get There
Turn off NH 16 just west of Conway onto the Kancamagus Highway. Six miles from this junction, turn right at the sign for the Covered Bridge Campground. Drive across the covered bridge over the Swift River. Turn right and watch for the sign for Boulder Loop Trail parking.

The Trail
In the parking area, a sign directs you to the trail, which soon forks. Bear left for the first of the information points—a rock, smoothed by the ages, extending 100 feet along the trail and reaching up 30 feet. Lichens grow on it much as they did when they were the first plants on the bare rock of the world.

At each stop you learn about glaciers, rocks, and trees. Along the trail through hardwoods and evergreens, you see examples of soil formation and forest origins from the time of the glacier 50,000 years ago: erosion, lichens and moss, elementary plants and trees, mature specimens of oak, spruce, fir, pine, hemlock, beech, maple, birch, ash, and various other trees native to the White Mountains.

You also see boulders, a rock slide, a brook, blowdowns from a northeast storm, fracturing granite, dry slopes with plants adapted to that sunny envi-

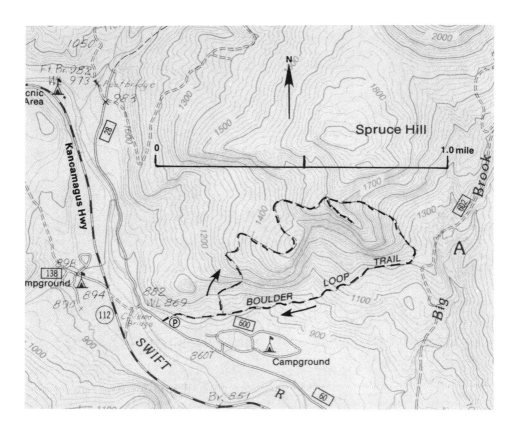

ronment, contrasting cool-moist slopes, and birds and flowers in season.

The trail takes you to a splendid outlook 1000 feet above the Passaconaway Valley. A spur trail leads to ledges giving views from the highest elevation. You see Mount Chocorua's sharp peak and the bulky Mount Passaconaway beyond the nearer forested ridges. These lookoffs have the built-in dangers of all cliffs.

Descending through the hardwood forest on the return half of the loop, you pass tall beeches. Watch for claw marks on the smooth gray bark. Bears climb in the fall for beechnuts.

4

Kedron Flume

Distance (round trip): 2 miles

Walking time: 1¾ hours

Vertical rise: 600 feet

Maps: USDA/FS 7½' Crawford Notch; USGS 7½' Crawford Notch

Crawford Notch is a pass through the mountains. For years it provided a route between the interior Connecticut River valley and the seacoast region. Discovered by hunters in the days when New Hampshire was a royal province, and explored by settlers following the Saco River after the Revolution, Crawford Notch became a teamsters' passage between sheer cliffs and steep forested slopes. The notch is a state park now. A railroad and US 302 wind through it. But, a short distance into the woods, the mountains are still primitive and rugged.

How to Get There
For a brief hike into this mountain fastness, take US 302 at the junction with US 3 in Twin Mountain and drive

about 11 miles through the notch's gateway crags to the parking area at the Willey House Historical Site. If you are coming from the east, drive about 18 miles on US 302 from the junction with NH 16 in Glen.

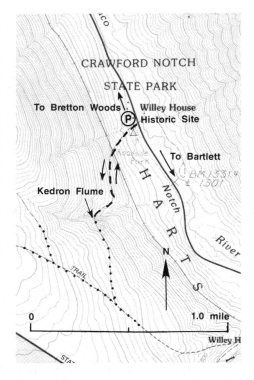

Kedron Flume

The Trail

The Kedron Flume Trail is to the right of the picnic tables, which are tucked into the steep slope. You start climbing immediately, following blue blazes.

The trail leads you to the railroad track near the site of the earth avalanche that wiped out the Willey family in the summer of 1826. As you approach the track, you'll see a trestle culvert, with moss creeping over stones and mortar. This Maine Central Railroad track was abandoned in 1984. But in 1995 the Conway Scenic Railroad began running trains through the notch. So the track is in use again, and you should be careful as you cross it to the trail's log-and-rock steps on the other side.

The trail continues steep. Although graded, with switchbacks, it is a mountain trail. The soft stone gravel will roll underfoot. Watch your step, especially descending. The trail leads through beech woods toward spruces farther on. It bends around a shoulder and dips into a little ravine at Kedron Brook.

The stream pours down through a narrow sluice or flume in the rock and drops over the falls below the trail's crossing. Remember rocks are slippery when wet. The outlook across the notch's gash is to Mount Webster's southern ridge and minor cliffs.

For 0.5 mile past the flume, the trail twists more steeply up among big spruces and rocks to its junction with the Ethan Pond Trail, a route into the Pemigewasset Wilderness past the Willey Range Trail up Mount Willey, which towers above Kedron Flume.

5

Three Ponds—
Brown Brook Loop

Distance (round trip): 5½ miles

Walking time: 3½ hours

Vertical rise: 500 feet

Maps: USDA/FS 7½' Mt. Kineo;
USGS 7½' Mt. Kineo

A hike to Three Ponds and across a height-of-land to another watershed on Brown Brook is a leg-stretcher and fine for gaining woods experience. At Three Ponds Shelter, you may cook hot dogs and beans at an open fireplace. (Carry out your trash!) A weekend in June is a good time to visit this forest environment of boggy ponds, beaver dams, hardwoods, and evergreens. Wildflowers, then abundant, will include pink lady's slipper, the little yellow flowers of clintonia, and carpets of Canada mayflower. White-throated sparrows give their haunting, north country whistles. Joining in will be all the returned birds.

But take plenty of fly dope. Black-flies will welcome you in June. Tuck long pants into socks. A head net is a wise precaution.

Be prepared for trail changes caused by beaver activity and blowdowns.

How to Get There
Drive along NH 25 west from Plymouth and turn north through Rumney, taking the Stinson Lake Road to Stinson Lake. Keep left along the west shore. The road changes to gravel. At 6.9 miles from NH 25, turn left at a hiker symbol, and park.

The Trail
The Three Ponds Trail leads into the woods across bog bridges over a trickle of water. Watch for yellow blazes. The trail continues uphill among maples and birches interspersed with hemlocks and pines. Near the middle of this hill the Mount Kineo Trail leaves on the right. You will return here at the conclusion of the hike.

The trail keeps irregularly along the west slope of Black Hill and takes you past the Carr Mountain Trail. About a mile farther you descend to a footbridge over Sucker Brook and join an old logging road, the former trail. Turn to the right on it. After another bridge, you make three bridge-less

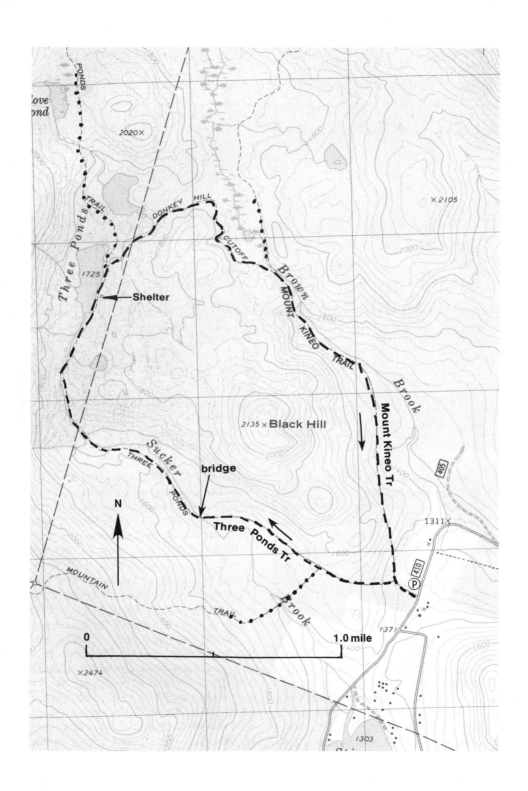

At Three Ponds

crossings of Sucker Brook; these may be difficult. As you approach the ponds, Middle Pond appears on your left. Watch for a path on the right up a steep bank. It leads to the Three Ponds Shelter on a knoll. South of it, hidden by trees and brush, lies the smallest pond, called Lower Pond. Hardly worth visiting, its area is 2.5 acres compared to Middle Pond's 13 acres.

The trail continues through the woods bordering Middle Pond. Toward the end of the lake, take a path right to avoid a boggy area. Shortly thereafter you come to a trail junction and sign. The Three Ponds Trail turns left. Straight ahead the Donkey Hill Cutoff will be your link to the Mount Kineo Trail and Brown Brook.

But before continuing on the Donkey Hill Cutoff, take a side trip to unique Third, or Upper, Pond. Turn left along the Three Ponds Trail. Cross an abandoned beaver dam; this may be tricky. The trail becomes a logging road for about 0.25 mile to Upper Pond. A hundred yards before the pond, the Three Ponds Trail branches left. You continue straight to Upper Pond. (The Three Ponds Trail traverses forest to the Hubbard Brook Trail and NH 118, about 4 miles away.)

The 12 acres of water at its deepest is 10 feet, or 4 feet less than the 14 feet for Middle Pond, but it floods into coves and boggy growths of waterbrush and evergreens. A gentle slope of woods on the south grows luxuriant wildflowers around old camp-sites of trout fishermen. Perhaps there'll be a swimming black duck suddenly beating aloft from the wa-ter, possibly a mink or beaver if you wait silently on shore and listen to the thrushes. After a heavy rain, you hear the falls splashing down the west ridge into the pond from tiny Foxglove Pond.

Return to the old beaver dam and junction with the Donkey Hill Cutoff. Turn left. The Donkey Hill Cutoff is rather obscure as it bears right through the grassy upper end of the drained beaver slough. Then it swings sharp left to take the route of an old logging road. Climbing slightly but steadily, you cross the imperceptible height-of-land and descend more abruptly toward the bogs and beaver flowages of Brown Brook. Avoiding this wet tangle, after a view toward Mount Kineo, the trail climbs a small ridge and turns sharply right, south. You follow up and down several ridges and valleys, then swing west around a spruce swamp to the junction with the Mount Kineo Trail. Here at ledges over which Brown Brook flows and tumbles down into lower hardwoods from the spruces,

the Mount Kineo Trail crosses to the far bank. (The Mount Kineo Trail heads northward over a shoulder of Mount Kineo 3.5 miles to a forest ser-vice road in the Hubbard Brook Ex-perimental Forest.)

Keep straight down Brown Brook on the Mount Kineo Trail. Had you been dropped blindfolded from a helicopter along it, you'd easily mis-take it for the logging road you fol-lowed near Middle Pond. It keeps to the west bank of the brook for about 1 mile, then bears away to the right as a woods trail. Watch for yellow blazes on trees.

This section of the Mount Kineo Trail leaves the valley of Brown Brook, climbing slightly across a ridge to the junction with the Three Ponds Trail. Turn left for the short walk down to your car.

The road from Stinson Lake con-tinues east through Ellsworth to NH 3 at West Campton. Not maintained entirely in winter, it is plowed past the Three Ponds Trail. Maybe you'll be considering this loop hike for a winter ski tour.

6

East Pond

Distance (Tripoli Road to East Pond and back): 3 miles

Walking time: 2½ hours

Vertical rise: 780 feet

Maps: USDA/FS 7½' Mt. Osceola; USGS 7½' Mt. Osceola; USDA/FS 7½' Waterville Valley; USGS 7½' Waterville Valley

In its simple wooded setting, with Scar Ridge and Mount Osceola's West Peak in the background, East Pond resembles many small, high lakes, which nestle among the ridges and mountains surrounding the more impressive and famous peaks. Yet each is individual, a special goal for a hike. East Pond covers 6.5 acres. Much of the shore is lined with rocks, or gravel and sand. Dead trees standing in places testify to the flooding caused by beavers who build their dams at the outlet and inlet. The water is cool and clear; it reaches depths of as much as 27 feet and provides shelter for speckled trout, which seem inclined to stay there.

Across Scar Ridge's spruce-grown slopes, green lines indicate the routes of old logging roads. Scrap iron and bolts lie in the sand near the pond's outlet, relics of dredging for diatomaceous earth years ago. A ditch guides the little brook to its drop-off into the valley. In late September, berries of several mountain ash trees cluster in scarlet splashes above the shore and against the ridge, making a Christmas-like display of green and red. In the spring, snow lingers in protected hollows. Hikers on Memorial Day may still find a melting drift near the outlet.

How to Get There

The East Pond Trail crosses Scar Ridge and 5 miles of woods between the Tripoli Road and the Kancamagus Highway. The shortest route to the pond is from the Tripoli Road, which leads east off I-93 at Exit 31. The Tripoli Road is better known as the access to the Russell Pond Campground. It connects with the upper end of Waterville Valley and NH 49.

Drive past the campground's entrance road on your left. About 5 miles from Exit 31, watch on the left for the forest service signpost marking the

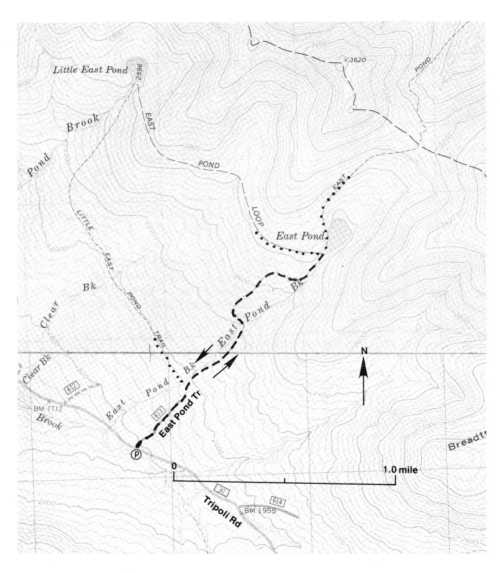

start of the East Pond Trail. Turn left and drive up to a parking area.

The Trail

The trail begins as a gravel road to a clear-cut 0.5 mile up the ridge. When the road bears right into that opening, keep straight on the old trail. After a few yards you come to the Little East Pond Trail on the left (see note at end of hike description), and you cross the railroad grade that once supported rails and trains servicing the Tripoli Mill to your right. Foundations still exist in the woods that grow from the site where the diatomaceous earth was processed.

Continue straight ahead as the trail rises gradually through hardwoods. Beyond the outlet brook you begin to climb more steeply for the remaining 0.5 mile into evergreens until the trail levels out at the pond. Its elevation is 2600 feet.

For hikers climbing over Scar Ridge to the Kancamagus Highway, the trail passes the south end of the pond and runs partway along the west shore before it swings away steeply and heads northeast for the height-of-land about 500 feet above the pond. Of course, a hiker crossing between the two roads must arrange transportation at the end of his hike.

Note about Little East Pond Loop: The Little East Pond Trail gives you the opportunity to see Little East Pond for 1 additional hour of hiking and about 2 more miles. At the south end of East Pond, where the East Pond Trail continues up the west side and a short right spur trail leads to the outlet, the Little East Pond Trail branches left (west) nearly on the contour for 1.5 miles, crossing small streams on the way to shallow Little East Pond. In contrast to East Pond's depth, here lily pads float on the surface above stems and roots long enough to feed on the bottom. The pads sometimes raise half their discs in response to the down-draft winds from Scar Ridge. Leaving Little East Pond, the trail follows the outlet at first, then at an abrupt left turn joins the old railroad grade that you crossed on the East Pond Trail. There you turn right for the brief descent to your car.

If the timing would suit you better for lunch at East Pond, hike the loop in reverse, from Little East Pond to East Pond.

7

Greeley Ponds

Distance (round trip): 4 miles

Walking time: 2½ hours

Vertical rise: 400 feet

Maps: USDA/FS 7½' Mt. Osceola; USGS 7½' Mt. Osceola

The west shoulder of Mount Kancamagus and Mount Osceola's precipitous East Peak frame the two Greeley Ponds in a wild and mountainous setting. The northern or upper pond below Mad River Notch reflects the western cliffs; the lower pond narrows between boggy shores grown to spruce and fir.

As an official National Forest Scenic Area, 810 acres surrounding Greeley Ponds are preserved in their natural beauty. To this end, the forest service has taken down the old log shelter by the upper pond, because, paradoxically, it was too popular. Sanitation problems, fuel requirements for the fireplace, garbage and rubbish disposal, and campsites extemporized nearby all despoiled the scanty earth, the pure water, and the slow-growing trees. People were overwhelming the delicate environment they had come to enjoy. So the forest service has asked overnighters to plan their trips elsewhere. Visit, but don't camp.

How to Get There

Take Exit 32 off I-93 and drive through Lincoln onto the Kancamagus Highway past Otter Rocks Rest Area and the forest service's trail sign for East Pond on your right. Don't turn off at the sign for the Greeley Ponds Cross-Country Ski Trail. Continue on to the next sign on your right, for the Greeley Ponds Trail parking. The distance from the exit to the parking area is 10.3 miles.

The Trail

Beyond a small knoll, the yellow-blazed trail leads over bog bridges across wet seepages. There may or may not be a bridge over the South Fork of Hancock Branch. Turn right after this crossing, following the blazes.

Then you climb easily to Mad River Notch, where the Mount Osceola Trail diverges on the right. Beyond this, avoid the cross-country ski trail marked by

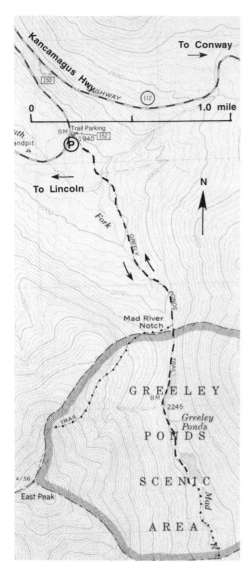

right a few yards, and begins intersecting the ski trail, which in summer is usually wet and muddy. After 0.5 mile you come to the lower pond. Unlike the upper pond, it is narrow and shallow. (The Greeley Ponds Trail follows the valley southwest 3 miles through woods of conifers and deciduous trees along the young Mad River to so-called Depot Camp in Waterville Valley, now a clearing at the beginning of the Livermore Road.)

The upper pond has an area of 1.25 acres and a maximum depth of 27 feet. The lower pond averages 3 feet deep over its 2 acres. Beavers seem at home in both ponds. As a beaver swims past, his brown head leaves a wake like a toy powerboat. Alarmed, he whacks his tail on the water and dives immediately.

You may want to return to eat your sandwiches by the upper pond. Spruces and pointed firs rise toward the cliff and reflect in the still water. Speckled trout break the surface to suck down hatching flies. Juncos and white-throated sparrows call from the trees. Cedar waxwings flutter over the pond to catch bugs, then return to a tree branch alongshore and preen their glossy feathers. Swallows skim above the spruces or dip into the pond for an instant of a skimming arc after insects. Dragonflies patrol the airways.

From the towering western cliff I once saw a peregrine falcon dive like a winged projectile at a black duck on the pond. The duck submerged at the last moment and escaped. The peregrine spread his wings and shot upward into hunting circles before giving up and flying off toward the lower pond area. The duck finally appeared cautiously in the brush along the west shore. This was in 1947 before the disastrous effects of DDT almost exterminated

blue triangles. Your trail drops a short distance to the upper pond and follows under the cliffs along the west shore in evergreens. Near the outlet, a spur trail, left, leads around the end of the pond to the former shelter site.

Straight ahead, the Greeley Ponds Trail continues past a spring on the peregrines, ospreys, and eagles. Now these raptors are recovering.

A Note on Overuse

The increasing popularity of the mountains creates a problem faced by the forest service, by the Appalachian Mountain Club, by other mountain clubs, and, in fact, by all conservationists and all citizens: overuse.

Hikers, like all mankind, congregate, and so destroy the primitive environment they seek. On Mount Washington, Tuckerman Ravine camping had to be restricted to protect the trees, plants, and soil; they are responding. In the Franconia Range, the Liberty Spring Shelter has been replaced by tent platforms. Campfire and camping regulations throughout the White Mountain

National Forest are being extended to preserve both the forests and the areas above treeline. The problem became so serious that the forest service established Forest Protection Areas (formerly called Restricted Use Areas or RUAs) to allow natural recovery of damaged land, trees, plants, and water. Soil erosion, vegetation loss, water pollution, compaction of soil, usually at campsites, are examples of environmental damage that hikers can cause. Excessive use of campfires and the accompanying destruction of the wood resource are in need of control also. Obviously, dispersal of hikers is necessary, and an important aim of the program.

Easy access to the mountains is certainly not the whole problem, but it may be part of it. The Kancamagus

Lower Greeley Pond

FRED BAVENDAM

Highway accounts in some measure for the popularity of Greeley Ponds and the consequent overuse, classification as a Forest Protection Area, and removal of the shelter. Camping and fires are prohibited year-round at Greeley Ponds and within a 0.25-mile strip on either side of the trail from the Kancamagus Highway.

Although Greeley Ponds had long been designated a Scenic Area to preserve its special beauty, this was not enough. The area is recovering, and I like to think that hikers are learning to be more careful of the forest and mountains. I am encouraged by the improvement in the litter along trails and at campsites. Hikers are responding to the motto "Carry In, Carry Out." They are also taking to heart more and more (I believe and hope) the ethics of good camping and hiking practices. You can do the same by following the restrictions in the forest service's "Backcountry Camping Rules." (See Introduction.)

With care and preservation, the mountains can be a continuing source of "wildness" in the deepest sense, of life force from the trees, moss, lichens, birds, and animals—but only if man controls his own "wildness."

8

Old Mast Road and Kelley Trail

Distance (round trip): 5 miles	

Walking time: 3¼ hours

Vertical rise: 1000 feet

Maps: USDA/FS 7½' Mt. Chocorua; USGS 15' Mt. Chocorua

The loop from Wonalancet over the Old Mast Road and the Kelley Trail connects with other trails between NH 113A and the Kancamagus Highway. The area offers hikes and climbs of varied distances and destinations in the Sandwich Range—mountains that extend west from Mount Chocorua and include Mount Paugus, Mount Passaconaway, Sandwich Mountain, and others north of the Lakes Region.

A hike need not be a physical challenge. Woods walking provides the satisfactions of escape and seclusion as well as the pleasures of striding and breathing deeply. For these purposes, the Old Mast Road–Kelley Trail combination is ideal.

According to legend, the Old Mast Road was first cut through the prime-val forest to haul out great masts for the British navy. The trail's ascent up even contours toward Paugus Pass, and the long stretches without a turn, would seem to bear out the legend. For contrast, the return route takes you scrambling down Cold Brook via the Kelley Trail. (If you are hiking with young children, it would perhaps be better to do the hike in reverse, so that their energy will be high for the rocks of the Cold Brook ravine.)

How to Get There
Drive to Wonalancet on NH 113A from Sandwich or Tamworth. Near the picturesque church, turn off NH 113A onto Ferncroft Road. Drive a scant 0.5 mile to a road on the right. Take it across the field to parking at a bulletin board.

The Trail
Walk along the road from the parking area to the woods. At a fork and gates, turn left onto the Old Mast Road and the Kelley Trail.

You soon come to a bridge over a brook. (The Wonalancet Range Trail starts up on your left for those wooded summits and the Walden Trail.) At 0.3 mile the Kelley Trail branches off

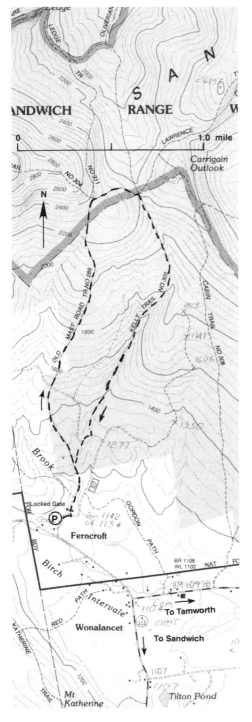

to the right. This will be your return route.

The Old Mast Road becomes an unused logging road up a steady grade. You climb through a forest of beech and yellow birch. The rugged, older, yellow birches have a reddish-brown-gray bark, scaly and furrowed, as though a different species from the younger trees with their pale yellow bark that peels across the trunks in ribbons and layers. Their leaves resemble those of the white birches sometimes growing near.

Easily distinguished are the smooth, gray, beech trunks common along the trail which they shade by extending their muscular branches almost horizontally. The branches end in slender twigs and light green leaves; the delicacy seems to belie their strength. The burrs enclosing the triangular nuts begin to open in late August, to the delight of squirrels and blue jays. Bears also feast on the beechnuts by climbing into the branches. Keep looking at the gray trunks and you'll see the healed gouges of claw marks—but probably no fresh ones.

During a warm damp August, many mushroom varieties appear almost overnight. There are both edible and inedible varieties, and, of course, some very poisonous ones. Among the toxic varieties are the deadly amanita, both the yellow type and the white species known as the Destroying Angel. Fragrant orange chanterelle, smelling of apricots when warmed in your hand, shaped like a little inverted twisted saucer on a stem, is a gourmet's delight. But, unless you are an expert on the various species, don't take chances by eating any of them.

Birds along the trail are typical of the deep woods, such as thrushes, although a scarlet tanager sometimes flits and calls among the high branches, or a fluttering redstart flashes among smaller trees.

After 2.5 miles, the Old Mast Road terminates at a junction on the height-of-land named Paugus Pass. Continuing north, descending, rough, is the Square Ledge Trail. Left, or west, the Walden Trail leads up Mount Passaconaway. Right, or east, the Lawrence Trail crosses the pass and climbs Mount Paugus. The Lawrence Trail also leads to the Kelley Trail. You are briefly in the Sandwich Range Wilderness.

Turn right (east) on the Lawrence Trail and follow it 0.5 mile to the Kelley Trail. At their junction, the Lawrence Trail continues its rough and steep ascent east up Mount Paugus. To the left (north) the Oliverian Brook Trail leads, after about 4.5 miles through wet ground along Oliverian Brook, to the Kancamagus Highway. For your return to Wonalancet, turn right (south) and follow the Kelley Trail into the ravine of Cold Brook.

Here the trail descends over bed-rock and past glacial falls and through gloomy, cool woods of big spruces. A ledge split again and again looks like the stonework of an expert mason. There may be deer tracks on the miniature sandbars, maybe a winter wren on a mossy log, trilling like a coloratura canary. Lush woodland ferns grow from dark humus and curve over rocks. Hobblebush blossoms are white in early summer—they turn to green berries later, then red. Graceful gray-green lichens thrive on ledges.

Lower down in the valley, the Kelley Trail stays on the west bank high above the brook, then descends steeply and crosses to the east bank. As you approach the last section of the trail, you come to a logging road. Turn right and walk up the road about 100 yards to a Kelley Trail sign and blue blaze on the left. The trail enters the woods and in 0.25 mile joins the Old Mast Road. Turn left and follow the Old Mast Road back to the parking area.

9

Belknap Mountain

Distance (round trip): 1½ miles

Walking time: 1¼ hours

Vertical rise: 740 feet

Maps: USGS 7½' Laconia; USGS 7½' West Alton

A short climb to the lookout tower atop Belknap Mountain opens a view across Lake Winnipesaukee's blue water and many islands. The Ossipee Mountains rise beyond in impressive array, green ridge upon green ridge forming a long single mountain from this distance. To the left, 50 miles away and unmistakable in spring and fall when it alone displays snow, Mount Washington appears distant yet splendid. Nearer and somewhat in line, peaks of the central and west Sandwich Range group themselves beyond the far end of Lake Winnipesaukee. Still more to the left and again distant, the line of rocky Franconia Range is dominated by Mount Lafayette. Foothills around Mount Moosilauke fill in the panorama continuing west. On a sunny day the passing high clouds

shift light and shadows upon the lake and mountains.

Of the four summits in this small, circular range south of Lake Winnipesaukee, Belknap Mountain is the highest, although perhaps not so well known as Mount Gunstock with its ski area of the same name. Mount Gunstock and Mount Rowe are usually climbed by trails from this ski area, where information is available. The fourth summit, Piper Mountain, is a bare ridge to the south. Belknap Mountain offers not only the highest summit, 2384 feet, but also a mountain drive to a picnic area.

How to Get There

Turn off NH 11A at Gilford onto the Belknap Mountain Road and proceed south through the village. At 0.8 mile the road makes a left turn and climbs to the top of a ridge; then at 1.3 miles it turns sharp right and continues south under the mountain slopes. At 2.4 miles from NH 11A, take a left onto the Carriage Road at a Belknap Mountain sign. Another sign warns you that the gate ahead is closed from 6 PM to 8 AM. The Carriage Road leads into a steep valley, winds upward, changes to gravel, resorts to switchbacks, and

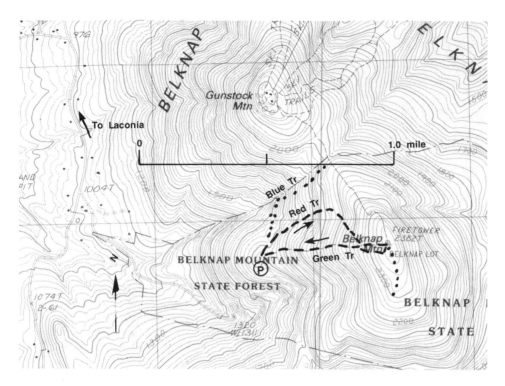

ends in 1.5 miles at a level parking area.

The Trail

For the trails to the summit, walk up-hill along the continuation of the road and past a small garage. A wide service route on the right goes up near the telephone and TV cable lines. This is the Green Trail, marked with green paint blazes, by which you will return. More pleasing to hikers is the Red Trail beginning on the right a few yards along a woods road. The path enters the woods and is identified by red paint blazes. It rises steadily and becomes more of a mountain trail as it bears right into spruces and passes an outlook to the west with a view of Kearsarge in the distance. Continue climbing uphill. Through the spruces you see sheds. The summit is directly beyond, surrounded by spruces; ledges support the steel tower.

Belknap Mountain is worthwhile climbing even on a hazy day. Although distant mountains are obscured, the nearer Lakes Region and Lake Winnipesaukee's varied shorelines appear in a bird's-eye view. The lake is busy with boats. There is activity and traffic on roads in the Laconia–Weirs Beach area. For contrast, the woods stretch away east to the bare summit of Mount Major. A pond at the east base along NH 11A shows that beavers have taken over an old hay field. Belknap Mountain's blueberries resemble packaged varieties in supermarkets, but a handful will remind you what blueberries are supposed to taste like.

Return to the parking lot easily by the service route, the Green Trail.

10

Plymouth Mountain

Distance (round trip, not including Pike Hill Road): 3 miles

Walking time (not including Pike Hill Road): 2½ hours

Vertical rise: 894 feet

Maps: USGS 7½' Newfound Lake; USGS 7½' Ashland

Like Stinson Mountain to the northwest, Plymouth Mountain's high ridge is especially suitable in the spring as an introduction to a season of climbing. Or you may want to visit it in the fall when the foliage is most colorful and when snow has already chilled the more northern peaks.

Plymouth Mountain, although visible from I-93 southwest of Plymouth, is little known and unspoiled. It is steep, yet undemanding. Because it rises in the Pemigewasset River valley and has a variety of trees and terrain, the slopes are alive in May with migrating birds. Sometimes the annual arrival of the warblers happens before the leaves unfold. Then you can spot the little birds clearly. The sum-

mit's evergreens and ledges attract juncos and white-throated sparrows. You see more birds than views because the ledges at the summit are surrounded by evergreens, which grow a little taller every year, but you gain a perspective up the beautiful valley leading to Franconia Notch.

Among the many birds, the black-throated blue warblers seem to favor Plymouth Mountain as late as the last 10 days of May after the leaves are fully out. Watch for the slate-blue back of the male, with the identifying touch of white on the wings, and the black throat above a white breast. His notes are an odd buzzing series with a rising inflection at the end. Trace the sound high up in the oaks and beeches, and you may catch the singer in your binoculars.

During this latter part of May, there will be little green carpets of dwarf ginseng, the leaflets topped with frilly white blooms. The occasional large oaks, beeches, and yellow birches have an undergrowth of lesser trees sheltering other wildflowers and ferns. This forest changes to spruce and fir along the ridge in a manner typical of these New Hampshire elevations, here reaching 2187 feet.

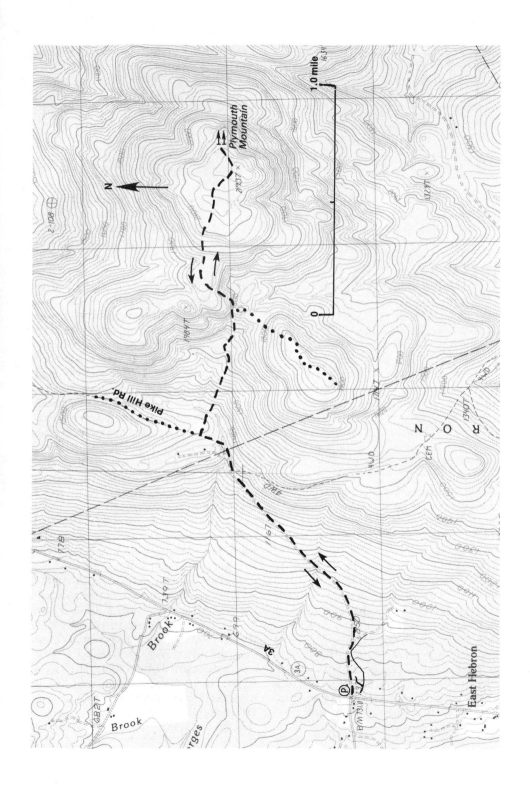

How to Get There

Follow NH 25 west from Plymouth. Turn south on NH 3A at the rotary and drive toward Newfound Lake. At 5 miles, watch for the right turn to Hebron and Groton, but don't take it. Opposite this, left, is a dirt road that looks like a driveway. It is Pike Hill Road. Although there may be a town sign warning that the road is not maintained for auto traffic and that users pass at their own risk, the road has been much improved. But parking and turning around at the trailhead can be a problem. So if you prefer, park on the wide shoulder of NH 3A and have a pleasant hour's walk uphill to the trailhead.

Following Pike Hill Road, bear left after 0.25 mile at the first fork. Next, a snowmobile trail branches left. Keep straight. At 1.2 miles you come to a contemporary ranch house on the left. Continue past the ranch house and red town line marks. After about 200 yards, keep right at the fork up the unimproved section of Pike Hill Road. At about 150 yards, watch for a brown wooden sign on a tree to the right proclaiming PLYMOUTH MOUNTAIN TRAIL. Opposite the trail, in the woods to the left, you can see an old well; a brick house once stood here.

The Trail

The markers put up by Camp Mowglis are little boards stenciled with a black wolf. The Plymouth Mountain Trail takes you first through a former logging yard and over a low rise. Beyond this you descend and cross a small brook. You then begin to climb steeply into a forest to the east.

Throughout the hike, look back and orient yourself for the return trip.

The trail makes a 90-degree left turn in a rock defile. Look for the trail sign up the steep slope on the left.

At about 0.75 mile, you come to a lookoff rock to the right, from which there is a tree-framed view of Mount Kearsarge and Newfound Lake. You'll also see the Ragged Mountain ski slope and Mount Cardigan.

Return to the trail. As you bear left up a ridge, don't be deceived by a bare ledge; it's only a false summit. But stop for the view that includes Mount Moosilauke, Mount Tecumseh, and the unusual sight of Mount Chocorua lined up behind Mount Israel.

The true summit is about 15 minutes ahead. Descend the rock slab, following the trail climbing again through spruces. Your route is now along the ridge to the summit cairn.

For the spectacular views, find the OUTLOOK sign and follow a spur trail to a large rocky area offering you enjoyment of the panorama—and lunch. The farthest mountain you're looking at is Washington. You can see the Franconia Range, Welch and Dickey, Tripyramid, Chocorua, Whiteface, Sandwich Dome, the Squam Lakes, Lake Winnipesaukee, and Lake Winnisquam.

Various cairns mark routes to other views, such as East Cliff, but use caution if you venture from the main trail. You can easily get lost.

Return the same way, watching for the right turn at a cairn as you descend the summit ledge. You'll understand the usefulness of the old woodsman's trick of looking behind for the return perspective.

(Note: Another trail, the Ken Sutherland Trail, has been constructed up the north side of Plymouth Mountain.)

11

Mount Major

Distance (round trip): 3 miles

Walking time: 2½ hours

Vertical rise: 1000 feet

Map: USGS 7½' West Alton

Steep, wooded slopes and ledges hide this bare summit (1784 feet) above Lake Winnipesaukee's Alton Bay. Mount Major surprises you with the extent of the outlook in all directions, but you are primarily attracted to the lake, for this is a lakeshore mountain.

How to Get There

The scenic highway section of NH 11 runs above the west shore of Alton Bay. A western ridge conceals Mount Major's flat crown. At 4.2 miles north of Alton Bay, a highway sign identifies the parking area for the Mount Major Trail.

The Trail

The trail, actually a logging road, enters a little valley of oaks, maples, and hemlocks. Almost at once it forks. Blue blazes direct you to the right. (The left fork rejoins at the top of the slope and displays an interesting gully eroded in rotten rock. You might like to take this alternate route during your descent.) The right fork rises steadily, blue blazes leading you upward.

Soon you follow a westering curve at the junction with the left fork. The road levels along the north shoulder of the mountain. Check your watch because your turn upward toward the summit is only 10 minutes away. Old stone walls parallel the road or strike off among the oaks.

Watch for blue-blazed arrows pointing left. Turn off the logging road and continue your climb on the true mountain footpath. It winds over rocks and among pines. It grows steeper. As you approach the first open ledges, you may notice several bypasses; they return to the trail blazed in blue on the open rock. In early June, there are pink lady's slippers flowering. Columbine blossoms beside the rocks. While you climb the ledges, pause to look behind you for the first high views of Lake Winnipesaukee.

Low-bush blueberries grow along the trail. Wild cherries, pines, young white birch, and mountain maple extend into the blueberry patches. The

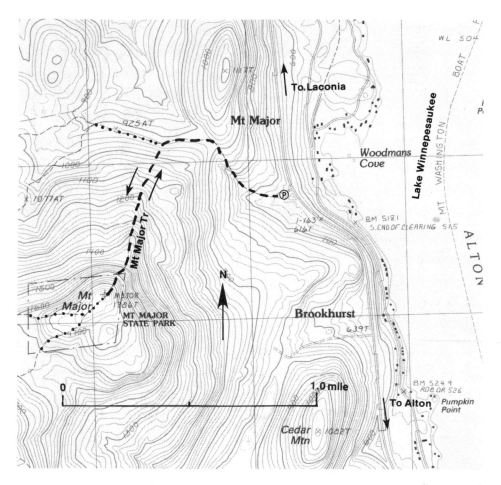

trail reaches the final ledges, which may look daunting to you. Use caution. These are at first sharp and in places sheer for a few feet, putting you to handholds and careful footholds. This is scrambling, not rock climbing. The upper ledges are worn away by glaciers and by exposure, but the coarse, notched surfaces are readily surmounted.

On the open summit, a four-sided stone shelter stands out against the sky. Roofless, its rock slabs, mortared into walls, were built in 1925 by George M. Phippen, a lifelong summer resident of Alton Bay. Winter winds took

off two roofs. From this landmark various outlooks open in all directions. The views sweep around you, but the lake catches and holds your attention.

Long and narrow, Alton Bay extends to the south. Northward the big lake stretches to the east shore and the town of Wolfeboro. Directly north is the length of Rattlesnake Island. Beyond, the blue water extends northwesterly broken by many islands and peninsulas, or "necks," which blend in the distance with the reaches of the lake and wooded slopes rising to the Sandwich Range and Ossipee Mountains. Often in summer, haze

Stone shelter on Mount Major

obscures the farther peaks, but on a day of real clarity you can see Mount Moosilauke, the tips of one or two Franconias, Sandwich Mountain, Whiteface, Passaconaway, and—rising behind Ossipee's long ridge—Mount Washington. To the west, Belknap Mountain's tower marks that summit, above lesser, forested ridges.

Mount Major, open rock except for blueberry bushes and small birches, exposes you to cooling breezes, welcome after the climb.

Descend by the same route.

12

Hedgehog Mountain

Distance (round trip): 5 miles

Walking time: 3½ hours

Vertical rise: 1300 feet

Maps: USDA/FS 7½' Mount Chocorua; USGS 7½' Mount Chocorua

Rising between the valleys of the Oliverian Brook on the east and Downes Brook on the west, Hedgehog Mountain at 2530 feet contains a variety of pleasures: a simple loop trail, woodsy walking, scrambling up ledges, and views both wide and fringed.

How to Get There

From the east, turn off NH 16 in Conway onto the Kancamagus Highway (NH 112) and drive about 13.6 miles. From the west on I-93, take Exit 32 in Lincoln and drive about 21.8 miles on the Kancamagus.

Opposite the Passaconaway Campground, you'll see a sign on the south side of the highway for the Downes Brook, UNH, and Mount Potash Trails. Turn here and drive in to the large parking area.

The Trail

A University of New Hampshire forestry camp in the area gave the UNH Trail its name. It swings left off the Downes Brook Trail after 60 yards. Follow the UNH Trail 0.2 mile to the junction of the loop. The fork to the right will be your return route down the western side of the mountain. Take the eastern route straight ahead. You are traveling clockwise, for the best viewing.

The first section of the trail, an old railroad grade, has the broad stateliness of a promenade, and it is an excellent warm-up for the hike. You walk along on pine needles, the forest glowing green and golden in the morning sun.

At 0.4 mile, bear right onto a logging road. Following the yellow blazes, you begin to climb, first gradually, then more steeply, through hemlocks and birches. At 1.6 miles you cross a brook in a ravine. On you climb, up over roots and rocks, and soon the trail begins to become exposed over ledges.

Then, at 2 miles, the east ledges spread out before you, with their views south and southeast. Be wary of some sheer drop-offs as you gaze at Mount

Passaconaway, Mount Paugus, Mount Chocorua, and the Moats.

Continuing onward, you see the summit ahead before you reenter the woods. The trail twists up and down until you are circling up under the boulders of the summit. Reaching the top at 2.9 miles, you have a closer view of the mountains you saw at the east ledges, as well as the eastern slope of Mount Tripyramid.

When you leave the summit, follow the yellow blazes. Views to the north and west open up through the trees, and if the weather is clear enough you can even see Mount Washington. You can also see the Presidential Range, the Carrigain Range, North and South Twins, Franconia Ridge, Mount Willey, and the Bonds.

This view is the feature of Allen's Ledge, which you come to at 3.7 miles, where a sign indicates a side trail to the ledge 60 yards to the right. And here again are Paugus and Chocorua. The ledge is named after Jack Allen, an early White Mountains guide.

Return to the main trail and continue down to a right turn onto a logging road, which will lead you to the loop junction and that grand promenade of the morning.

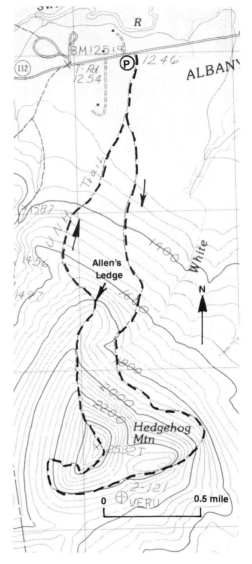

13

Stinson Mountain

Distance (round trip): 3½ miles

Walking time: 2 hours

Vertical rise: 1390 feet

Maps: USDA/FS 7½' Rumney; USGS 7½' Rumney

Alone and easily accessible from the Baker River valley, Stinson Mountain has the specialties and charms of smaller mountains. Its elevation of 2900 feet treats the hiker to the joy of arriving at the summit after just enough effort and distance to impart a sense of accomplishment. This delight, compounded of well-being, good luck, and the wide view, has more to do with why people climb mountains than the commonly accepted motive "because it's there."

The summit ledges, once the site of a fire tower, offer fine views, although the views to the north are now partially obscured by trees growing up. Forests, mountains, and lakes surround the lovely rural valley along Baker River with its farms and houses. The Franconia Range and the Sandwich Range are north and east. The village of Rumney lies at the foot of the mountain, Stinson Lake in the hollow to the north, Campton Bog to the east. Lesser-known mountains on the west—Mount Cube, Smarts Mountain, Piermont Mountain, Carr Mountain—are clothed in forests. To the north, Mount Moosilauke rises above treeline.

Pleasant and varied in any season from spring to late fall, Stinson Mountain is especially fine in October, not only for the trail, which rises through leafed woods of red and yellow, but for the blends of colors spreading out in all directions from the summit. By then the cone of Mount Moosilauke is sometimes snowcapped.

How to Get There
Drive west from Plymouth on NH 25 to Rumney. Turn north through the village to Stinson Lake. Bear right near the outlet of the lake at the sign for Hawthorne Village and continue uphill 0.8 mile to the sign for the Stinson Mountain Trail. Swing to the right onto a road less traveled and drive 0.3 mile to parking on the left at the start of the trail.

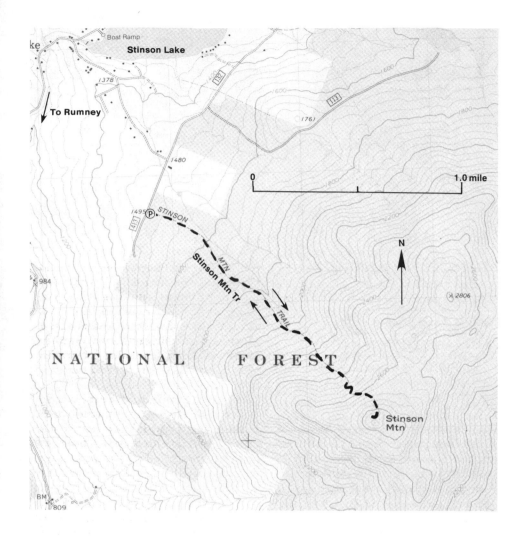

The Trail

Blazed yellow, the trail leads into open woods and along stone walls to an old cellar hole, which it passes on a left corner. Large trees grow from the cellar, demonstrating the many years since (probably) the roof of the farmhouse fell in after the family moved west or became city folks.

The trail ascends gradually to a trickling brook. Here you begin the real climb by turning right and going up the steep slope. Alternately switching from steep grades to easier old logging roads, the trail passes a narrow opening with a view over Stinson Lake and toward Mount Moosilauke. Entering spruce and fir woods interspersed with striped maple and mountain ash for the last climb, the trail curves right and breaks out all at once into the clearing at the ledges.

14

Mount Cardigan

Distance (around the loop): 3½ miles

Walking time: 2½ hours

Vertical rise: 1220 feet

*Maps: USGS 7½' Mt. Cardigan;
USGS 15' Cardigan*

A crown of solid rock forms the top of Mount Cardigan. As you approach the fire tower lookout exposed to the open sky and wind, you are taken by the illusion of climbing on the barren rock of some remote and mightier mountain; instead you are on an outpost of the White Mountains at only 3121 feet elevation. The illusion is dispelled by the sight of initials and dates carved in the rock over the years. Cardigan has been a popular climb for a long time, and many trails ascend it.

The route of this hike is a loop from Mount Cardigan State Park's parking and picnic area up the West Ridge Trail, and return via South Peak and the South Ridge Trail. Access roads approach through the towns west of the mountain, Canaan and Orange.

Cardigan's distinctive rock dome is extended by the lower ledges of the north and south ridges. The rock is known as Cardigan pluton. It is a form of Kinsman quartz monzonite common in New Hampshire and is part of a formation at various levels, 60 miles long and 12 miles wide, extending from West Peterborough to north of Groton.

Here on Cardigan, forest fires destroyed the trees and organic earth, and erosion exposed the bare rock. In 1855, a fire twisted up in flame and smoke from the north ridge so spectacularly and with such destruction that the rock is still largely barren, and the ridge is named "Firescrew," from the spiraling smoke and flames that were visible in all the villages for miles around.

The south ridge is also open rock, with only scattered evergreens. Views from South Peak are mostly east and west. But pick a clear day. Summer haze, which spoils the view, can sometimes be avoided by making an early morning climb.

About the first week in May, the lower forested slopes of hardwoods show the greenery of new leaves while trees above are still bare or only budded. In the fall, the first yellow and

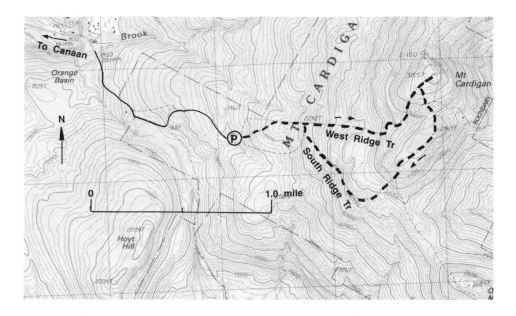

red leaves appear near the summit, while the lower trees remain green. Changes requiring weeks at a single elevation appear in one glance down the mountainside.

Also, in spring and fall, watch out for ice on the rock. You could slide a long way into the trees with time to think about other errors before the crash.

Growing below the South Peak's ridge in May will be dogtooth violets—really members of the lily family—and small yellow violets, purple trillium, and wood anemone. In summer look for the flat leaves of the green-flowered orchis.

Binoculars are useful to study the lakes and farther ranges, or to peer into towns, or to watch a raven near the summit. This bird from the north has been seen on Cardigan. Warblers flock to the wooded slopes at migration time.

The summit receives the full blast of the wind. If the fire warden is in on a windy day, a climb to the lookout gives you an unbelievable "ride." The glassed-in room seems to rush downward with a rocking, roaring rumble, straining against the cables. In a high wind, the room sounds and feels like a subway car.

The view, starting west and looking counterclockwise, extends to Vermont, then Massachusetts, then east over the New Hampshire Lakes Region and the Belknaps, and around to the northeast, where the Sandwich Range is moored by the pinnacle of Mount Chocorua. Perhaps the clouds swirl over the distant Presidentials and Franconias. Mount Moosilauke, northward, may be impressively white in early spring and late fall. To the northwest where four townships meet by Bryant Pond, a ridge running south is scarred by old mica mines.

How to Get There

To reach the west side of the mountain and the West Ridge Trail, drive to Canaan on US 4. Turn north on NH 118, and soon take a right at a sign for Mt. Cardigan State Park. Drive into Orange, following the Cardigan signs 4.1 miles to the parking area and picnic tables.

The Trail

The West Ridge Trail leaves the picnic clearing at a sign on the edge of the woods and climbs by easy stages. Keep left past the South Ridge Trail, which offers the best views as part of the return loop. Watch ahead frequently for the trail's orange blazes; especially keep a sharp eye open when you approach one of the numerous branching paths that are not your route.

Walk past the Skyland Trail, which is a ridge route to Alexandria Four Corners. The West Ridge Trail crosses a footbridge, leads past the site of the old shelter, passes two branch trails, and ascends steeply over rock, along a route identified by cairns and orange paint to the lookout tower.

In descending, go down to the lookout's cabin, bear right from the junction with the Clark Trail, and take the South Ridge Trail. At the next trail signs, turn left for South Peak and Rimrock. The trail leads you over partially wooded ledges beyond South Peak with its great views, to Rimrock, and then crosses the Skyland Trail. It descends steeply and slabs around through woods to the West Ridge Trail at the junction you passed on the way up, 0.5 mile above the parking area.

15

Smarts Mountain

Distance (round trip): 6 miles

Walking time: 4½ hours

Vertical rise: 1938 feet

Map: USGS 7½' Smarts Mountain

Although only 3238 feet in elevation, Smarts Mountain provides excellent views from its now disused steel fire tower. You look up and down the Connecticut River valley and over into Vermont. Northern mountains extend all the way to the Presidential Range.

On July 13, 1993, Doan family members and friends and the Dartmouth Outing Club trail crew gathered at the Smarts Mountain trailhead in Quinttown for the dedication of the Daniel Doan Trail. Dan himself was too ill to attend, but his words were present as Earl Jette, the director of Dartmouth College Outdoor Programs, read Dan's description of the hike from the first edition of *50 More Hikes in New Hampshire*. Then an orange DOC sign with the new trail name was nailed up. Dan was toasted with sparkling cider, and everybody sat down to a picnic.

At his home in Jefferson, New Hampshire, Dan took great delight in hearing the details of the ceremony, and he was deeply touched by the dedication, which was made "in recognition of Daniel Doan's efforts to stimulate interest and involvement in hiking and the out-of-doors."

Dan loved Smarts Mountain, the second mountain he climbed as a boy, after Cube. In the early editions of *50 More Hikes in New Hampshire,* he wrote a backpacking loop using this old unnamed trail along Mousley Brook to the summit for an overnight, then down via the Ranger Trail to the Lyme-Dorchester Road and back by the Quinttown Trail. "I'm a former Orford resident," he explained, "so I naturally recommend the approach from that side, where the north slope rises from a valley of deserted farms known as Quinttown."

But in 1991 he decided he should change the loop to the more accessible trailhead in Lyme Center for the Lambert Ridge Trail and the Ranger Trail. This is the backpacking Hike 47 in the current *50 More Hikes in New Hampshire,* and in it Dan tells tales of his boyhood adventures on Smarts.

Now the trailhead in Quinttown is

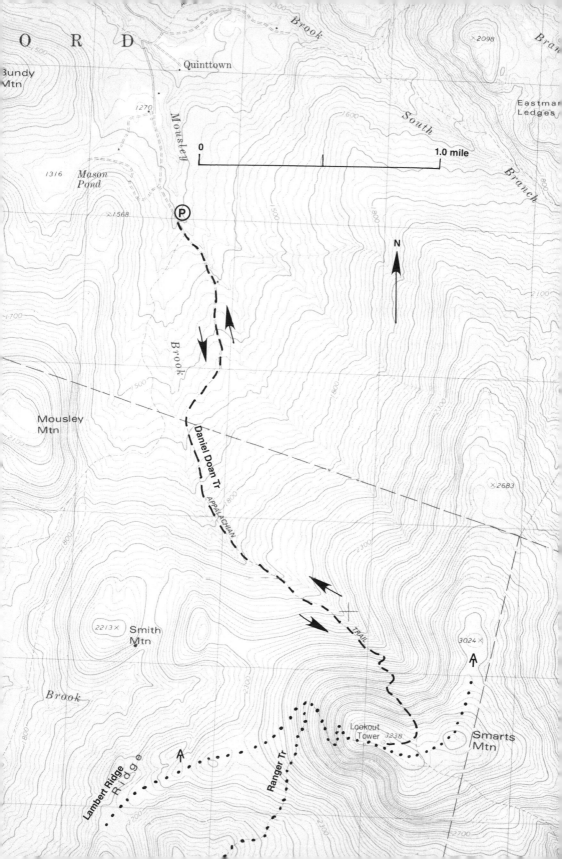

easier to find, thanks to clear road signs into this area of abandoned farms, where there is a pervading sense of the past that inspired Dan's novel *Amos Jackman,* set in a fictionalized Quinttown in the 1930s.

The following description of the Daniel Doan Trail incorporates Dan's description in the early editions of *50 More Hikes in New Hampshire.*

How to Get There

Coming from the east, turn off in Wentworth onto NH 25A. At about 10.5 miles, watch closely on the left for a road sign: QUINTTOWN ROAD. Coming from the west on NH 25A, drive 1.6 miles past the store in Orfordville and watch for the sign on your right.

Turn onto the Quinttown Road, which climbs southeast along the north bank of Jacob's Brook. There's no village at Quinttown now, and the old farmland—some of it first cleared by Benjamin Quint who served during the Revolution as a sailor under John Paul Jones—has largely returned to forest. What once was Quinttown is now just an intersection.

At 1.8 miles you'll see a sign for the Mousley Brook Road. Turn right, crossing a bridge. At a T-shaped fork in the road, you are facing the site of the former schoolhouse. Bear right. The road twists up steeply in a hairpin turn, to the left, and continues uphill through woods. Then it levels through open fields and pastures, with an old barn on the right and a great view of Smarts.

After 2.6 miles from NH 25A, you reach the small parking area on the left.

The Trail

Walk down the road, across a bridge, straight to the orange DOC sign at a fork. To the right is the old Quinttown Trail to the Lyme-Dorchester Road 5.1 miles away. Ahead is the Daniel Doan Trail.

Walk ahead past the camp on your left. At a fork, take the trail to the right. Do not go left across a snowmobile bridge.

For most of the first 2 miles the Daniel Doan Trail ascends gradually. This is an early farm road, as indicated by old apple trees and stone walls. These woods were open fields grown with brush when Dan first explored them.

You leave this area for higher valley forests along Mousley Brook. The logging done there apparently did not disturb the black bears, who probably now outnumber the people in Quinttown. During the time of ripe shadbush berries, about the first week in August, bears leave tracks in the mud of the trail and break off branches from the small trees in greedy attempts to reach the berries. Don't worry about meeting a bear. He'll be long gone before you come anywhere near him . . . except perhaps after a rain, when the combination of quiet footing and a wind in your face might prevent your sounds and scent from preceding you.

At 1.3 miles, look for a blue blaze on your left where the trail bypasses a short eroded stretch. Take this bypass. The old trail will soon rejoin it, coming in on your right.

The logging road has kept to the north of Mousley Brook as far as the base of the mountain. There, at 1.7 miles, it crosses to the south bank and begins the real ascent for the 1.3 miles to the summit. The climb alternates between short, steep sections and older, contour-following sled roads.

Finally you are climbing on a moun-

Ruth at Dan's trail

tain trail over rocks and roots. They can be slippery. White birches give way to spruce and fir. Leveling, the trail swings right. It passes on log bridges over a boggy area draining from Murphy Spring. Boreal chickadees have a liking for these evergreen woods. You climb out of the spruces into a small clearing around the old fire warden's cabin.

Continue on to the fire tower and climb it. From the tower you look across the Connecticut River valley to Vermont where you see Mount Ascutney southward, Killington and Pico southwest, and Camel's Hump and Mount Mansfield northwest. Turning to New Hampshire you look north and east over nearby Mount Cube's quartzite-frosted summit. Then there are Mounts Carr, Stinson, Kineo, Moosilauke, the Franconia Range, and finally Washington.

Dan always looked northwest into Orford. He selected a domed hill called Sunday Mountain. (As a child, he thought it was so named because it was shaped like the scoop of ice cream in a sundae.) Then on its shoulder, Dame Hill, he located his first farm, where he raised chickens in the 1930s.

To the south, under the steep brow of the mountain, Reservoir Pond gleams. Cummins Pond lies to the east along the Lyme-Dorchester Road. To the southwest there are the Dartmouth Skiway's slopes and lifts near Holt's Ledge, and farther south, Moose Mountain in Hanover.

After enjoying the view and your lunch, return to the Daniel Doan Trail for the descent. Shortly after crossing the brook, bear right at a fork. Then continue on down to Quinttown.

FRANCONIA NOTCH REGION

The view pushed me. I sank down on a rock and tried to sort out some detail from the total wildness. The silent splendor was too simple for the word, just trees really, but it brought me a shiver.

—Daniel Doan
Our Last Backpack

16

Artist Bluff and Bald Mountain

Distance (round trip): 1½ miles

Walking time: 1¼ hours

Vertical rise: 400 feet

Maps: USDA/FS 7½' Franconia; USGS 7½' Franconia

Franconia Notch, with its state park and famous profile, two lakes, the tramway, and ski trails, all bordering the I-93 parkway, has too many attractions for a quick visit. Don't try to see all the lakes, streams, precipices, and rock formations in a day. Along with Cannon Mountain, Eagle Cliff, and Mount Lafayette, they are overpowering. First, get a hiker's perspective. If time is short and the urge to escape speeding cars and wandering tourists is imperative, climb Artist Bluff and Bald Mountain at the north end of the notch. You need only an hour or two.

How to Get There
Stop and look at the profile—New Hampshire's unique Old Man of the Mountain. Then continue driving north on the Franconia Notch Parkway past the tramway and its cable cars. Take Exit 3 onto NH 18, which soon brings you to the parking area for Echo Lake Beach. Leave your car there.

The Trail
The trail to Artist Bluff starts on the north side of NH 18. Walk back east from the parking area. The trail is on your left near a highway route sign and west of the outlet from Echo Lake. Climb the highway embankment by a path worn in the gravel. At a sign for the bluff the trail enters the woods and leads up among big rocks. There's a steep climb up a gully.

Near the top, at the junction with the trail to Bald Mountain, continue straight ahead on a spur trail a few yards to Artist Bluff. This is a rock cliff from which artists might paint the notch, but it's more often a vantage point for photographers. The view is magnificent across Echo Lake to Eagle Cliff and Mount Lafayette, left, and to Cannon Mountain on the right.

For a complete hike above the north and western gateways of the notch, return to the trail and turn right. Climb the remainder of the gully and over the wooded height above. The trail leads up and down over the knolls. You pass another ledge lookoff before you descend to the sag below Bald Mountain's summit. Watch for the tall old spruces along the trail. Most of them have been struck by lightning, and their trunks bear the vertical scars. The trail joins a former carriage road up from NH 18. Turn right for Bald Mountain. Climb the trail by a series of steps over rock from the first switchback.

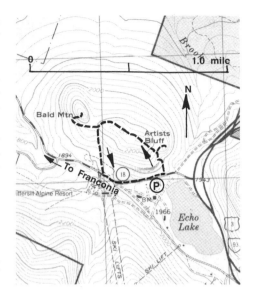

On the rocky open summit you stand clear of the small spruces. You look west over Franconia village, far away to the Connecticut River valley, and into Vermont. Cannon Mountain's ski slopes are south. Turning around left, you look into the deep notch, again across Echo Lake.

Return to the junction with the Artist Bluff Trail. Turn right and follow the trail down the graded, ancient carriage road to NH 18. It ends at the parking area for skiers on the Roland Peabody Memorial Slope. Keep left across the parking area and walk beside NH 18 back to the Echo Lake Beach parking area.

View from Bald Mountain

17

Mount Pemigewasset

Distance (round trip): 3½ miles

Walking time: 3 hours

Vertical rise: 1170 feet

Maps: USDA/FS 7½' Lincoln; USGS 7½' Lincoln

Mount Pemigewasset, at the south end of Franconia Notch, is the buttress for the Indian Head, whose impassive profile looks down upon the motels and restaurants along old US 3 and to I-93 curving to the south. The summit's cliff-top also has views of peaks far and near. The mountain extends north from the cliffs forming the Indian Head, and the trail to the top in that direction starts near the parking for the Flume Visitors Center. The open ledges at the end of the climb give the mountain an individuality that is more spectacular than its height would suggest, for its elevation is only 2557 feet, less than half that of Mount Lafayette 5 miles away to the northeast.

After the tourist attractions of the notch, you'll be refreshed by this climb above the parkway and by the view of the mountains and valley. At sunset, you watch the horizon glow, and you are treated to a much rarer sight: the low-angled shadows and the brilliancy of the late sun on the peaks of the notch, a series of gleaming crests above the purple valley.

It will be time then to return to the highway and your car. For a sunset hike, take a flashlight with new batteries and a picnic supper in a small knapsack. If you linger on the mountain, you will find that the twilight of the summit has changed to darkness in the valley.

In the days of mountain inns, instead of returning to a parked car, you would have crossed a lawn to the lights and hospitality of the Flume House.

How to Get There
Take Exit 1 off the Franconia Notch Parkway. As you drive into the Flume Visitors Center, bear left to the north end parking area. The Franconia Notch Bike Path has its southern end here. Leave your car and walk up the bike path about 100 yards to a sign on the left for the Mount Pemigewasset Trail.

The Trail

This gravel path soon takes you through an underpass below former US 3, now called the Flume Service Road. Turn left over a footbridge and follow the trail through hardwoods to a second underpass, and then to a third, completing your passage under the parkway. You might pause to admire the intricate stonework of granite facings on the concrete underpass.

Two hundred feet upward takes you into a forest of beech, maple, yellow birch, white birch, and other deciduous trees. The trail swings to the right and begins slabbing the contour, where it has been dug into the slope or provided with stone steps. You cross three small brooks on bridges of three flattened logs. After the third log bridge turn left up a steep rise. You are on the old trail that existed before the parkway and Flume Visitors Center.

Here the climb really begins, but along a curving, moderate route among the great trunks of ancient beeches and maples. At one corner you will face a particularly massive beech. Look up at the claw marks in the smooth, gray bark. A black bear, one fall, climbed up this tree to reach the beechnuts in the branches. Both large and small black bears have this urge and capability. Keep watching as you move on and you may find other beeches with claw marks, although I doubt if you will find any recent, unhealed scars. Bears have five toes and five claws, yet usually only four show on the trees. The little toe on the inside of the paw (unlike the human toe arrangement) does not often dig into the bark.

Steady climbing lifts you to the north side of the mountain in a growth of spruce and fir. The Indian Head Path comes in on your right; continue ahead. The almost level trail follows for a short distance the edge of a wooded dropoff on your right. Three yards of upward scramble put you into a green tunnel with a stone floor. On a good day, you emerge with blinking eyes into bright sunlight. The slant-

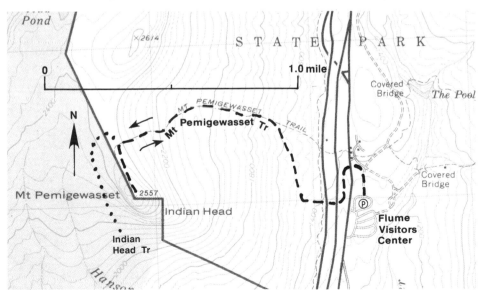

ing ledge ends in emptiness and distant mountains. With trees at your back you are standing beside the scalp lock of the Indian Head. Here is the place to bring wandering children under control.

The view immediately ahead below the cliff is one of both forest and human enterprise along US 3 and I-93. To the right, a leafy forest turns brilliant yellow, red, and orange in early October. It stretches away to a swampy area along Harvard Brook known as Bog Eddy. Beyond this and bearing northwest you see the cut of a power line, then farther away the triangular shape of Mount Wolf. The Kinsman Ridge Trail traverses that mountain as a section of the AT. (See *50 More Hikes in New Hampshire,* Hike 46, Gordon Pond). The long ridge to the southwest is Mount Moosilauke, the westernmost of the White Mountains.

Looking to your left you'll see the ski trails on Loon Mountain east of Lincoln. Beyond and to the right is Mount Tecumseh; to the left, Mount Osceola, now without a fire tower. Together they form the north wall of Waterville Valley. For a complete eastern view, follow the ledge in that direction, keeping along the fringe of evergreens on your left.

Walk upward to the left and step onto the lookout ledge for the Franconia Range. From the south northward the peaks are as follows: pointed Mount Flume and its massive slide, then somewhat nearer Mount Liberty with its stepped rock summit, next Mount Haystack all rock and sun and cloud shadows. Below it is the top of the vast rock sheet called Shining Cliff so very visible from Lafayette Place. The next is Mount Lincoln. Then comes the highest of them all, Mount Lafayette, and just to the left, the dome of North Lafayette.

Franconia Notch appears as walls of rock framing distant sky. The walls are Eagle Cliff to the right and the rock-climbers' playground, the expanse of cliffs on Cannon Mountain, some crags of which form the Old Man, although the famous profile is not visible from here. The summit of Cannon Mountain is capped by the little block of the tram terminal.

Pointed evergreens in front of you form delicate ornamentation against the panorama—and in time may grow up to obscure it. At present the green tips give the view a truly northern setting as a final reward for you as you turn around and descend the way you came.

Overlooking the Pemigewasset Wilderness

ROBERT J. KOZLOW

18

Basin-Cascades Trail

Distance (to Cascade Brook Trail and back): 2½ miles

Walking time: 2 hours

Vertical rise: 500 feet

Maps: USDA/FS 7½' Lincoln; USGS 7½' Lincoln; USDA/FS 7½' Franconia; USGS 7½' Franconia

Of the various trails maintained in the notch by the New Hampshire Division of Parks, the Basin-Cascades Trail is one of the most interesting. It passes through woods of fine stature, and it climbs up beside falls, pools, and rock formations along the way.

The Basin-Cascades Trail may be considered a link from the Basin to Cascade Brook Trail, which leads on to Lonesome Lake, but for hikers exploring the notch it is an experience in itself for an afternoon in mountain woods.

How to Get There
If you're driving north on the Franconia Notch Parkway, the exit for the Basin is about 6 miles beyond Exit 32 off I-93, to Lincoln. Heading south, you'll see the Basin exit about 3.6 miles from Cannon Mountain.

The parking at Basin East gives access by a footpath and an underpass to the Basin and this trail. Southbound parking at Basin West offers paths leading down beside the infant Pemigewasset River to the same waterfall and 20-foot pool. From either parking area proceed as directed by signs. The Basin demonstrates in a reduced flow how water and stones from a melting ice sheet bored the cavity in solid granite 15,000 years ago. The geological name is *pothole*.

The Trail
For the Basin-Cascades Trail turn back from the viewing area, cross a footbridge over a tributary stream, and enter the woods on a gravel path. Avoid taking paths to the left or right. Your trail's sign appears just beyond a right fork to another bridge and a path across a little hollow to a sign for the Pemi Trail. (The Pemi Trail leads north 1.5 miles along the west side of the river to Lafayette Place.) The Basin-Cascades Trail bears left after its sign, which is about 250 feet from the Basin.

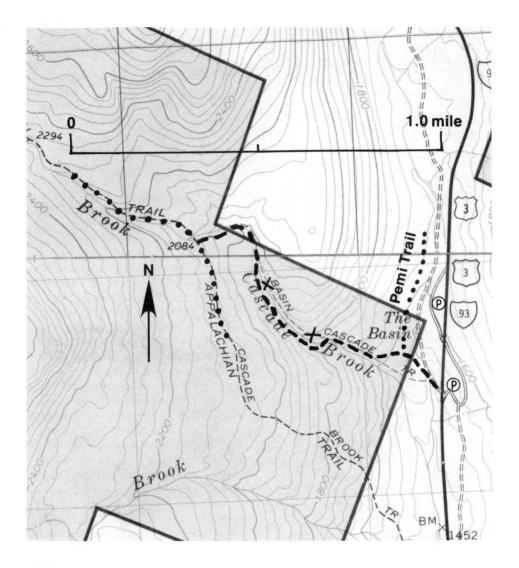

At a slight incline you approach the north bank of Cascade Brook. Blue-blazed, the trail steepens and is often rough, laced by exposed roots, and at times muddy. The much-worn path branches with informal spurs to the left for views where the brook slides over smooth ledges.

Signs on trees announce that you are at the boundary of the White Mountain National Forest, and con-sequently will leave behind the Franconia Notch State Park. The history of the park explains why you are hiking in such a magnificent forest. In the 1920s these trees very nearly fell to the logger's ax and saw. The Society for the Protection of New Hampshire Forests aroused people to the danger. Old-timers, who were children then, may remember giving a dollar—perhaps assisted by their parents—for a tree, in the society's campaign, Buy a Tree and Help Save the Notch. Major contributions came in from philanthropists, who would now be called conservationists or environmentalists. Women's clubs, newspapers, and the AMC contributed, as did New Hampshire taxpayers through their legislature, which appropriated half the $400,000 required to buy the 6000 acres along 7 miles of Route 3. On September 15, 1928, the Old Man of the Mountain overlooked the preservation ceremonies held at Profile Lake. The park was dedicated to the New Hampshire men and women who had served the nation in time of war.

Continuing up into the national forest, the Basin-Cascades Trail becomes less steep but remains just as rough. Keep uphill under fine hemlocks to Kinsman Falls. After rain, this cascade through chutes in the rock becomes a broad sheet of water sluicing over a vast expanse of smooth granite. Below the falls the trail crosses the brook on rocks. This crossing is dangerous at high water. Under any conditions it may deter casual adult walkers and families with small children.

Across the brook, the blazes change to yellow, then back to blue. The trail climbs steeply and continues to follow the brook through evergreen woods. Scrambling in places is necessary. Tree roots have been exposed by erosion and boots. The spruces shadow the brook so that Rocky Glen Falls appears as a glistening in the branches ahead. Keep left at the base of the falls and enter a chasm with damp rock walls. When you climb out of it and bear right you are above the falls and again beside the brook. A few yards farther on your left you pass the broken timbers of a footbridge. Soon you reach the end of the Basin-Cascade Trail at its junction with the Cascade Brook Trail. This section of the Appalachian Trail connects the parkway at Whitehouse Bridge (or more exactly former bridge), the Whitehouse Trail from the Flume Center, and the Liberty Spring Trail, to Lonesome Lake west of you.

Day hikers with the time and energy to visit Lonesome Lake may follow Cascade Brook Trail, but there is no bridge, and at high water the crossing can be dangerous. Follow Cascade Brook Trail 1.5 miles to the lake and the AMC hut there. (See Hike 19.)

Those who turn back from such a long round-trip of 5.5 miles can enjoy the descent along the same Basin-Cascades Trail, saving the excursion to Lonesome Lake for another day. Returning on the trail you've been going up shows you the woods and streams in a different light and perspective, so in a sense it becomes another trail. Cascade Brook rushing down the mountainside may not seem to be plunging toward the sea, but it surely is, and will return as water vapor in clouds to again drench these mountains and replenish this lovely brook.

19

Lonesome Lake

Distance (round trip): 3¼ miles

Walking time: 2¾ hours

Vertical rise: 1000 feet

Maps: USDA/FS 7½' Franconia; USGS 7½' Franconia

One thousand feet above Franconia Notch is Lonesome Lake, a goal for climbers and visitors who take advantage of the graded trail to walk in and see a true mountain lake in a spectacular setting. No longer "lonesome," quite the opposite, the much-used trails, along with the plywood hut of the AMC and the voices of hikers with their colorful packs and clothes, give a modern touch to the ancient scenery.

The lake has been popular since the days of mountain inns after the Civil War. The trail still mostly follows the old bridle path, along which many vacationers from the now-vanished hotels rode to the lake for the magnificent view of the mountains on both sides of the notch.

Legend names President Ulysses S. Grant as one of the notable visitors. According to the story, he came to the notch and the Profile House in 1869. A yellow coach and six bay horses driven by Ed Cox, a famous "whip," brought him from Bethlehem in 55 minutes—a fantastic rate of more than 13 miles an hour. In later years, a steam train and rails brought guests to the Profile House, which burned in August 1923.

The views from Lonesome Lake are, indeed, great—comprehensive, craggy, wild, and dominated by the treeless peak of Mount Lafayette. From the lake, trails lead to Cannon Mountain, Mount Kinsman, and Kinsman Pond. The Appalachian Trail passes by the lower end of the lake.

As many as 46 hikers can be accommodated at the AMC's Lonesome Lake Hut, situated on the west shore facing the Franconia Range. There is a trail around the lake, 0.75 mile, passing the site of old log cabins. A stand of tamarack makes a fine display of yellow in the fall. The lake is 2734 feet above sea level. Westward, the evergreen forest rises to the ledges of Mount Kinsman.

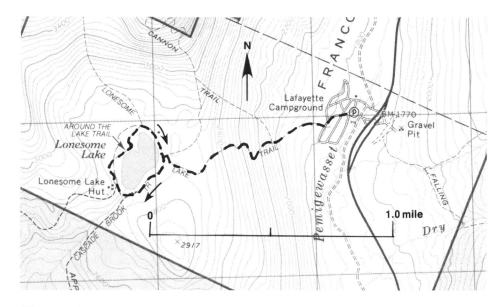

How to Get There

Your destination is the Lafayette Place Campground. Northbound on the Franconia Notch Parkway, note your mileage as you pass Exit 1. Continue on the parkway about 4 miles to an exit sign: TRAILHEAD PARKING. Smaller signs list the Bridle Path and Falling Waters Trail, but this exit is also for the Lonesome Lake Trail.

Leave your car in the parking area and walk through the foot tunnel under the parkway to the west side. When you emerge from the tunnel, bear left around the log cabin. Farther on you'll see a sign on your right for the Lonesome Lake Trailhead. Continue to the end of the south parking area.

(Driving north on the parkway, you will see a sign before the Trailhead Parking exit that tells you to take the Tram exit for the Lafayette Place Campground. If you plan to head south after your hike, you may want to park here at the campground instead of in the east side trailhead parking area.)

If you are southbound on the Franconia Notch Parkway, take the exit for the Lafayette Place Campground and Trailhead Parking, about 2 miles south of the exit for the Cannon Mountain Tramway.

The Trail

The Lonesome Lake Trail begins with a footbridge over a brook, which is the infancy of the Pemigewasset River. Follow yellow blazes and signs past the campsites. Leaving the campground behind, you proceed into the forest of tall hardwoods.

No-strain climbing limbers your legs. Not far beyond a left corner and two small bridges, you pass by the Hi-Cannon Trail on your right. This is about 0.5 mile from your car. Now the trail lifts you upward by the switchbacks originally designed for horses and riders. You may note the slope's steepness and welcome the angling path that you follow. The ridge, which looked so easy from Lafayette Place, seems to have deceived you.

ROBERT J. KOZLOW

Lonesome Lake

But the trail soon begins to level out, and after about 1 mile you detect a slight descent. The lake is ahead in its flat wooded setting. You come to a trail junction. Pause here and study the trail sign and the numerous trails listed. Orient yourself to the map. Even look behind you to familiarize yourself with the trail you've been on, so you'll recognize it when you return to it.

To reach the AMC hut, take the Cascade Brook Trail, which branches left from the Lonesome Lake Trail.

Follow along the east shore of the lake until you come to another trail junction at the lake's south end. Turn right on the Fishin' Jimmy Trail across the outlet, and take the left fork to the AMC hut.

For the return route, walk the Around-Lonesome-Lake Trail on the west shore to a junction with the Lonesome Lake Trail north of the lake. Turn right. Keep past the Cascade Brook Trail, and you are on the way back down to Lafayette Place.

20

Mount Flume

Distance (round trip): 10 miles

Walking time: 8 hours

Vertical rise: 3367 feet

Maps: USDA/FS 7½' Lincoln; USGS 7½' Lincoln

Appearing as a rocky pinnacle to the drivers and passengers northbound on I-93 and US 3 beyond North Woodstock, Mount Flume sets the style for the Franconia Range. This southern terminus of the long ridge above treeline is a fitting introduction to Mount Liberty, Mount Lincoln, and Mount Lafayette. But Mount Flume has its own distinction, namely, its rock slides and exposed ledges. These and the trail to the summit for this hike—the Flume Slide Trail—require a brief explanation.

Perhaps you have turned into the Flume Visitors Center for information and for a careful view of this mountain. From the parking area you may stare aghast at the obviously impossible face of the peak. Despite the

trail's name it surely can't lead up that. It doesn't—not exactly. The name refers to an earlier slide off to the right, now mostly hidden in trees that have grown on the original gash. It's formidable enough, however, so don't visit the famous Flume Gorge on the same day you hike.

How to Get There
Take Exit 1 off the Franconia Notch Parkway. As you drive into the Flume Visitors Center, bear left to the north end parking area.

The Trail
At a sign saying BEGIN BIKE ROUTE, follow the asphalt bike path and the Whitehouse Trail about 20 minutes to a bridge over the Pemigewasset River. Here the Cascade Brook Trail joins from the left. Beyond the bridge, watch on the right for the Liberty Spring Trail 200 feet farther along. You leave the bike path at this point.

The Liberty Spring Trail, a section of the AT, takes you up fairly steeply through a leafy forest, and in 0.5 mile to a sidehill fork. Keep right onto the Flume Slide Trail. (The Liberty Spring Trail continues toward the Liberty

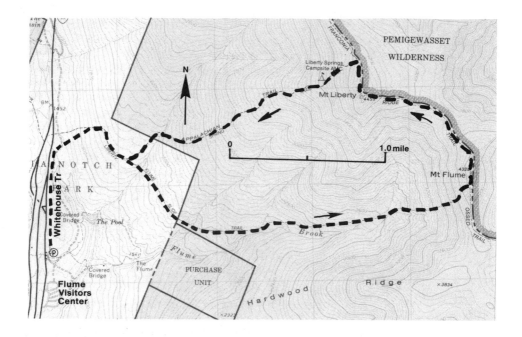

Spring Campsite and Mount Liberty. It will be the lower section of your return route.)

Taking the Flume Slide Trail from this junction, you begin a pleasant woods walk south and east for almost 3 miles to the base of the mountain. The trail follows a series of old logging roads and crosses various tributaries of Flume Brook. As you approach the base of the slide the trail can be altered annually by spring freshets. Watch for the blue blazes.

The challenge of Mount Flume begins at the slide. For more than 0.5 mile, you face the side of the mountain where once an avalanche of rocks and gravel poured down. Now grown to small birches and evergreens, it still keeps your eyes focused on footholds and handholds. Caution is required. Double your care if rain has soaked the rocks. Pause for the views opening across the notch to Mount Kinsman and Cannon Mountain.

At the top of the slide keep left as the trail enters spruces and firs, climbing to the junction with the Franconia Ridge Trail. At the right, the Osseo Trail leads south and east to the Lincoln Woods Trail and the Kancamagus Highway almost 6 miles away.

Follow the Franconia Ridge Trail left up into the spruce scrub to the edge of the open cliffs that you saw from the Flume Visitors Center. The trail skirts the edge, not a good route for anyone troubled by heights, although the scrub on the right can comfort and assist. A few yards north, however, is the summit of the peak, a small area of rock. The effect is immediate: a sense of achievement and emergence from a hard climb to an extreme height. Elevation, 4328 feet. The panorama is grand in all directions.

Northward you see the barren and rocky crests of Mount Liberty, Mount Lincoln, and Mount Lafayette, highest in the range. Turning west, you look across the notch to the humped summits of Mount Kinsman, and, at the head of the notch, Cannon Mountain bulking above the profile's cliffs. To the east, your eyes sweep over the forested valleys draining into the Pemigewasset River's East Branch. The far ridge in the Pemigewasset Wilderness rises north from cliffs to Mount Bond's treeless summit. Mount Carrigain, farther east, bounds the wilderness with its massive pyramid topped by an observation tower.

Continue on to Mount Liberty, down and up about 1.1 miles north along the Franconia Ridge Trail. Beyond the peak, turn left down the Liberty Spring Trail and descend to the Whitehouse Trail for completion of the loop back to your car. (See Hike 21, Mount Liberty.)

Note: Many hikers now prefer to take the relocated Osseo Trail, via the Lincoln Woods Trail, to Mount Flume. It is longer, about 11 miles round trip, but more pleasant, with an excellent view into the Pemigewasset Wilderness from a shoulder on the approach to the ridge.

21

Mount Liberty

Distance (round trip): 7½ miles

Walking time: 6 hours

Vertical rise: 3100 feet

Maps: USDA/FS 7½' Lincoln; USGS 7½' Lincoln

The ledgy crest of Mount Liberty lines up with the higher Franconia Range northward and provides closer views of the notch from a better angle than Mount Flume. Instead of a slide for a final approach, the Liberty Spring Trail leads up past a campsite popular with Appalachian Trail hikers.

A day pack with suitable equipment is necessary. The topmost crags can be cold and windy.

How to Get There

The climb, like the one up Mount Flume (see Hike 20), begins at the Flume Visitors Center. Take Exit 1 off the Franconia Notch Parkway. As you drive into the Flume Visitors Center, bear left to the north end parking area.

The Trail

Take the bike path and the Whitehouse Trail. After about 20 minutes, you'll cross the bridge over the Pemigewasset River. A few yards beyond, watch for the Liberty Spring Trail on the right. It leads you along a short level section before you start the 0.5-mile climb to the fork where Flume Slide Trail branches right. Keep left, as the Liberty Spring Trail continues up through the hardwood forest and crosses a brook. When water is high, this crossing may be difficult.

Steadily rising, the trail takes you up slopes once logged and burned. In 1917, hikers climbing among rocks scorched bare by a forest fire followed signs nailed to blackened stubs.

The trail swings up steeply to your right, then becomes more gradual, and passes Liberty Spring Campsite. (No shelter here; tent platforms only. Last water.) On up through the spruce/fir woods you climb to the Franconia Ridge Trail. Turn right (south) and follow the Franconia Ridge Trail up into the open, where you see the steep rocky summit ahead. You feel that lift of excitement from the expanse of

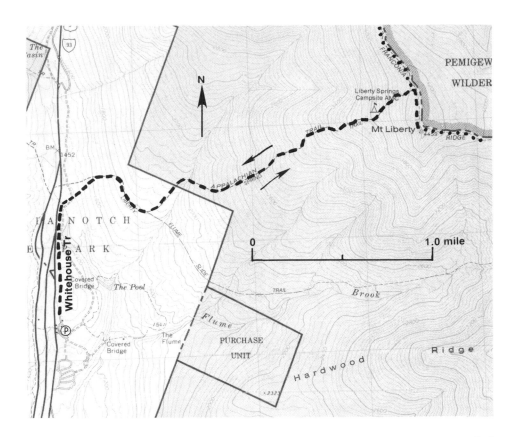

sky and mountain, and from the certainty that you'll soon surmount the last rocks.

This 4459-foot peak overlooks the great forests to the east in the Pemigewasset Wilderness. Northward, along the Franconia Ridge Trail, your gaze adjusts to the increasing height beyond Little Haystack Mountain, where narrow ledges rise to Mount Lincoln. On the left a distant green ridge curves down from the AMC's Greenleaf Hut into the notch below Mount Lafayette, which Mount Lincoln obscures. North, across the notch, the high cliffs of Cannon Mountain appear chopped from the wooded summit. Westward, Mount Kinsman's

slope and long summit ridge parallel the highway. In the opposite direction, east, Owl's Head, more like a great whale, fills the valley north toward Mount Garfield. Over Owl's Head, past Mount Guyot, the peak on the northeast horizon is Mount Washington. And all around, distant under a clear sky and high clouds, the mountains seem endless.

Often, however, Mount Liberty is in cloud, and the wind is cold. But luck favors the prepared hiker. If you carry, in a pack, plenty of extra clothing and a rain parka, maybe you won't need them; then you can sit in the sun and enjoy your sandwiches.

The descent takes you north along

View north from Mount Liberty

the Franconia Ridge Trail on the same route you climbed. Turn left onto the Liberty Spring Trail, and continue to the bike path and the Whitehouse Trail, which you follow back to your car.

22

NOT FOR THE FAINT OF HEART (OR KNEES) RUGGED CLIMB & DESCENT. IF THE WEATHER IS GOOD, PLAN ON SPENDING TIME ON THE "RIDGE". WELL WORTH THE EFFORT. TAKE <u>WARM LAYERS</u> & EXTRA FOOD!

Mount Lincoln

Distance (round trip, Mount Lincoln only): 8 miles; (around the loop, Lincoln and Lafayette): 8¾ miles

Walking time (Mount Lincoln only): 5¾ hours; (around the loop): 7½ hours

Vertical rise (to Mount Lincoln): 3350 feet; (around the loop): 3750 feet*

Maps: USDA/FS 7½' Franconia; USGS 7½' Franconia

To many hikers along the Franconia Ridge Trail, Mount Lincoln is a way station on the high line of peaks knifing north and south above Franconia Notch east of I-93. But Mount Lincoln can be a fine destination in itself. During the ascent, you will see spectacular waterfalls; a unique slanting cliff; alpine-arctic environment above treeline; and wide, wide views, especially overlooking the Pemige-

*Mount Lafayette is only 171 feet higher than Mount Lincoln, but the climb from the col north of Mount Lincoln is 400 feet.

wasset Wilderness clear away to Crawford Notch and Mount Washington. This hike offers the added bonus of a climb up the highest peak in the Franconia Range, Mount Lafayette, if you wish.

How to Get There

Leave your car at Lafayette Place midway of the state park. Here the Franconia Notch Parkway divides for a short distance into northbound and southbound lanes. Parking for either lane is connected to the other by a pedestrian underpass. The trail starts at the east or northbound parking. The campground, picnic area, information, and ranger cabin are near the west or southbound parking.

The Trail

Your trails for this hike leave the east parking to the left of the AMC information booth. The Old Bridle Path and the Falling Waters Trail coincide for 0.25 mile. At the bridge over Walker Brook they separate. Turn right across the brook onto the Falling Waters Trail. You leave this stream, which flows from a ravine of the same name on Mount Lafayette. (The Old Bridle Path keeps straight for a short distance before

Franconia Ridge from Mount Lincoln

ROBERT J. KOZLOW

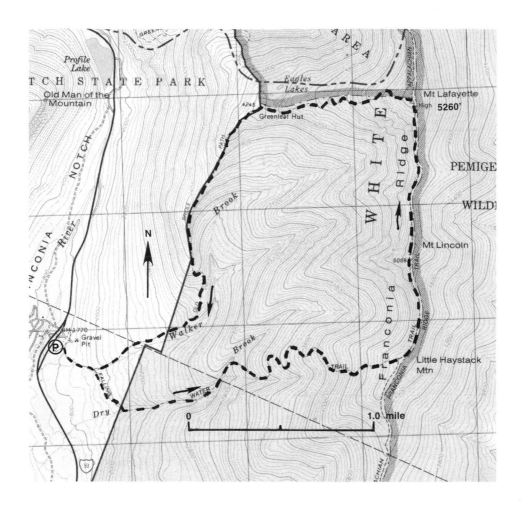

bearing left to join the former route before construction of the parkway. If you choose the loop for this hike, the Old Bridle Path will be your descent trail.)

Along the Falling Waters Trail you ascend gradually, swinging through woods of maple, beech, and yellow birch for another 0.5 mile to Dry Brook. Contrary to its name, the brook is a crystal torrent in early summer.

You cross Dry Brook to the south bank and begin a steeper climb. You pass cascades on the left and approach ledges high up in the trees. The trail

appears to end at a pool in a narrow ravine. Swiftwater Falls gushes into the pool from a ledge 60 feet high. You see the trail to the left of the falls. You cross to the opposite bank over rocks at the foot of the pool.

The climb begins here in earnest, although the trail is graded, and sections of it follow old logging roads. You were impressed by Swiftwater Falls. Now Cloudland Falls, 20 feet higher, descends toward you in a white, shifting curtain sliding into the gorge.

Above Cloudland Falls, from the steep and slippery ledge, you first look out across the valley. Following the AMC signs, cross to the south bank and then cross back to the north bank. The trail continues up rough and steep as the brook branches into the upper growth of spruce and fir. The trail takes you up a series of traverses between steeper pitches to a left turn at a junction. Here a sign indicates the spur trail 100 yards to the right, which leads down to the base of Shining Rock Cliff. This massive expanse of smooth granite angles up at a rounded 45 degrees for 200 feet to your left. It extends four times that across the ridge. It gleams in the sun when wet from the drainage off its brow of evergreens. Don't try to climb it. From your parked car at Lafayette Place in late afternoon you can see it really shining.

Back at the junction with the main trail you may wonder how much farther it is to the alpine-arctic environment I promised you. You'll soon see a sign: WELCOME TO THE ALPINE ZONE. In the next 0.5 mile the trail clears the scrub of treeline in a steep ascent into the open rockery of Little Haystack, a minor peak on the Franconia Ridge Trail.

If the wind blows rain, and clouds are setting into a blinding fog, this is a good place to turn back. Wait for a better day. The exciting panorama from the ridge demands a clear view. There's no value in a memory of Mount Lincoln as gray rocks packed in cotton batting. Besides, the ridge is dangerous in stormy weather. Lightning strikes frequently. Winds can be icy even in summer. You will be almost a mile up in the sky. The col between Little Haystack and Mount Lincoln is exposed, narrow, and in places almost sheer on each side.

In fine weather, turn north along the Franconia Ridge Trail and enjoy the 0.75 mile above trees in the open exposure of sun and sky. The summit of Mount Lincoln is at 5089 feet.

Multiplicities of mountains rise in all directions, and on the east the rocks fall away to green forests along Lincoln Brook and Franconia Brook, which flow around 4025-foot Owl's Head anchored like a humped barge in the green sea of trees. For a loop and return to your car, the Franconia Ridge Trail provides a clear-day bonus. North, beyond Mount Lincoln's summit, the trail descends, over and among rocks, all in the open, then up to Mount Lafayette's rugged slopes and summit cairn—a 1-mile hike among alpine-arctic plants, such as diapensia, hugging the windswept ledges. From Mount Lafayette turn left and go down by the Greenleaf Trail to the AMC's Greenleaf Hut. Then take the Old Bridle Path for the descent along a ridge where, in June, the rhodora blossoms are showy pink above Walker Ravine. The Old Bridle Path takes you to the junction with the Falling Waters Trail at the bridge over Walker Brook, and then to the east parking. If you don't choose to include the loop to Mount Lafayette, you may return from Mount Lincoln as you climbed and enjoy once again Shining Rock Cliff, Cloudland Falls, and Swiftwater Falls.

23

Mount Lafayette

Distance (round trip): 7¾ miles

Walking time: 6½ hours

Vertical rise: 3500 feet

*Maps: USDA/FS 7½' Franconia;
USGS 7½' Franconia*

The "top of the world" in the Franconia Range is, of course, named for the French hero of the American Revolution. His 1825 visit to New Hampshire brought about the change from the peak's older name of Great Haystack. Its northwestern cliffs and slides form the east side of Franconia Notch above Profile Lake. Its long, forested slopes of beech, yellow and white birch, and maple rise steeply from the parkway. Far up among the spruce scrub and barren rocks of treeline are two small lakes and the Greenleaf Hut of the AMC. The dwarf trees and ledges extend to a rockstrewn slope, 1 mile long, leading up to the summit at 5260 feet, with rare mosses, plants, lichens, and grasses along the way.

The exposed stones of the peak could be in the arctic rather than the temperate zone. Even on a summer day the wind often blows bitter cold. Plants are balanced on a delicate ecological margin. The dwarf spruces lie down before the wind and seem to grasp the rocks. Although doused with rain and fog, the mountain cranberry and similar creeping plants are thick-leaved against dehydration from the wind. The leaves of the low shrub, Labrador tea, curl along the edges and are woolly underneath, thereby retarding evaporation of vital leaf moisture in the harsh winds. These mountain vines, prostrate bushes, and shrubby heaths blossom white, pink, and purple in early summer.

Mount Lafayette has long been a popular climb. The oldest trail, still called the Old Bridle Path, was more than a name once. Travelers rode up it on mountain ponies from the Lafayette House, which burned in 1861. Only foundation stones remain of the vanished summit house, too, which in those days accommodated the successful climbers.

When the AMC built Greenleaf Hut, burros bore loads up the path and each year continued to transport supplies early in the season. Then, before the days of helicopters, the regular

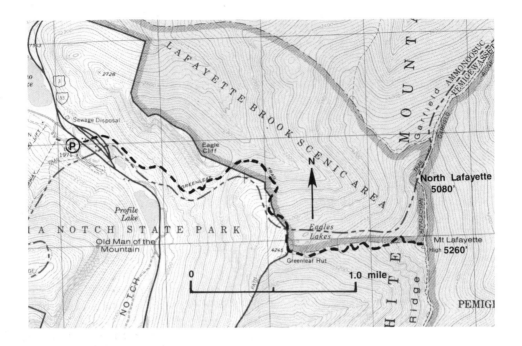

summer packing of necessary food and fuel depended on the legs and lungs of the hutmen lugging the long packboards. Still today, you will see "croo" members treading upward under heavy loads.

The Old Bridle Path, leaving the parkway from the east side at Lafayette Place, is the scenic route up Lafayette. The views of the upper ridge and of Walker Ravine open out from a partially wooded shoulder halfway up to Greenleaf Hut. Starting as it does at the same point as the Falling Waters Trail, described in the Mount Lincoln climb, the Old Bridle Path forms a pleasant and easy link in that loop. (See Hike 22.)

A northerly and more challenging route from Franconia Notch up Mount Lafayette, the Greenleaf Trail, mounts beside Eagle Cliff and reaches the north slope through Eagle Pass, 1000 feet above the notch, and opposite the profile.

How to Get There
Driving the Franconia Notch Parkway, take Exit 2 for the Cannon Mountain Tramway and Old Man Viewing. Park at the south end of the area for the tram. You'll see a Greenleaf Trail sign.

The Trail
With above-treeline equipment in your pack, walk across the access road to the tram and follow the sidewalk back to the parkway and through the underpass. Turn left up the exit road and then cross it to the sign for Greenleaf Hut on your right.

Climb the bank into the growth of hardwoods and at once swing to the right as the trail begins a slabbing route south, parallel to the parkway. Use care following it across the tailings of a slide. Soon, farther on, among rocks that rest in the forest from earlier falls, you join the trail that before 1987 began nearer Profile Lake. You are opposite the Old Man, which is hidden by leafy branches in summer.

Follow the blue blazes up steeper to a left turn and a series of switchbacks. From one corner you look down on the upper rocks of the slide you crossed below. Then the trail bears right. The footing is excellent and continues so on the upper trail as it curves north into Eagle Pass. You enter the pass under a long cliff similar to those towering still higher above. You pick your way over massive rocks as large as cottages, which have lodged in the pass. Snow and ice linger late in the gloomy caves below the boulders. If you leave the trail to explore, watch out for treacherous patches of moss over the crevices. The trail itself is safe enough.

Beyond the rocky confines of Eagle Pass, the trail turns sharply right and up moderately among slabs and imbedded flat rocks. The forest is mostly evergreens mixed with white birch and mountain ash. The trail zigzags to ease the steepness, along with occasional stone steps and waterbars. You are climbing a ridge high above Lafayette Brook on your left. Across the ravine an opening in the trees gives a glimpse of a towering dome—North Lafayette. The grade remains steady to steeper switchbacks.

Then the trail enters a nearly level corridor in scrub. You step out be-hind Greenleaf Hut and look beyond to the open views and alpine barrens above treeline, east to the summit. The glacial age is long gone, but the ice scoured the rocks before it melted away, leaving the great shards scattered precariously, a random and extravagant use of paving stone for men to wonder at.

Near the hut, the Old Bridle Path joins the Greenleaf Trail. You descend beyond the hut to the dwarf spruces again, then pass through the moist section at the little bog draining from the two basins of the Eagle Lakes. You climb above treeline once more and follow the worn pathway over the rocks. Massive cairns mark the route, which swings north for the final ascent.

If there's a storm brewing, turn around and leave the mountain to the lightning and thunder. If there's a clear hour ahead, watch the high clouds and their shadows moving across the mountains. Don't try to count the peaks. There are too many. Look east at the miles of green trees, and remember that before the days of the national forest the valleys were a blackened devastation of logged and burned ridges.

Return by the same route, the Greenleaf Trail, turning right, north, at the hut for the descent to Eagle Pass.

24

North Lafayette

Distance (round trip): 9 miles

Walking time: 7½ hours

Vertical rise: 3360 feet

Maps: USDA/FS 7½' Franconia; USGS 7½' Franconia

After you've surmounted (and recovered from?) the highest and most popular climbing summit in the Franconia Range, a very different day awaits you on its north shoulder. From a rocky dome, sometimes called North Lafayette, you'll gaze at Mount Lafayette to the south half a mile away and in a rarely seen perspective across a wide bowl of rock slabs and talus. A remoteness from the crowd on Lafayette's barren summit will emphasize the vastness of the mountain. You may even savor a mood of detachment, of isolation, which is a bonus for climbing this peak.

Of course it's not really isolated. The Garfield Ridge Trail crosses it at an elevation of about 5080 feet. (The Garfield Ridge Trail traverses north from Mount Lafayette to the AMC's

Galehead Hut, a difficult 6.5 miles of the AT.) This trail above treeline, with its white AT blazes, will be your final 0.25 mile southward after 4.5 miles up the Skookumchuck Trail from US 3.

How to Get There
The Skookumchuck Trail begins from the east side of US 3 at a parking area for the north end of the Franconia Notch Bike Path. Approaching from the south, drive through the notch on the parkway. Beyond the transition to I-93, take Exit 35 for US 3, and park on the right in 0.6 mile. Southbound on US 3, drive 0.25 mile past the junction of NH 141, and the trailhead will be to your left.

The Trail
The trail leads into the woods from the north corner of the asphalt. Blue blazes mark the uphill for 100 yards to a curve southward. At 0.1 mile, the trail crosses a wider trail, the Heritage Trail and a snowmobile trail combined. Ascending moderately before leveling off, the Skookumchuck Trail remains within hearing distance of I-93 traffic, whose roar diminishes gradually as the trail bears southeast. Still marked by blue blazes, the trail crosses

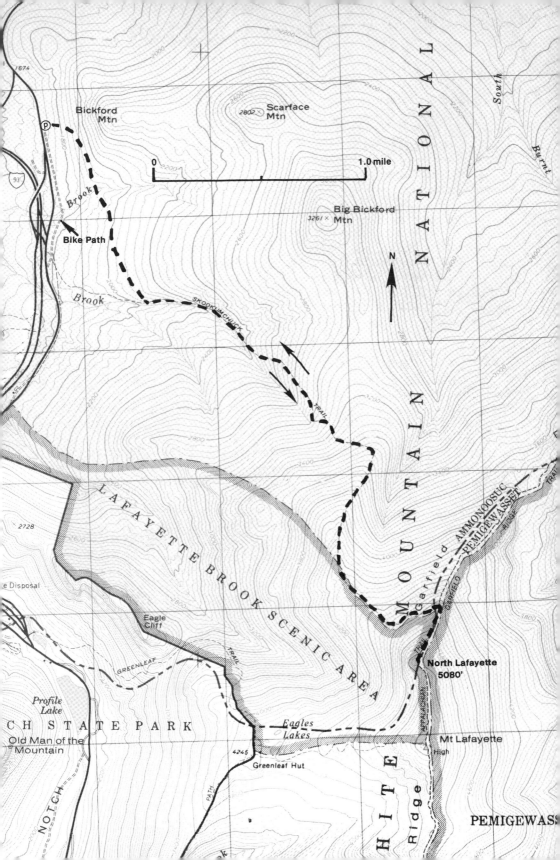

a small brook and continues up and down over several seasonal trickles. Soon you look into a little valley and hear the rippling of Skookumchuck Brook. The trail descends at a long slant to join the old trail leading upstream along the north bank. This completes your traverse of the new section necessitated by I-93 construction. You are 1.1 miles from your car.

Skookumchuck Brook, flowing steadily in its green valley, is very satisfying to walk beside. The original trail, gouged into the sidehill with log corduroy and crude bridges, tested one's ability to judge the depth of mud. In 1979 crews added stepping stones and split-log walkways. The bank on your left becomes higher and steeper as you walk, making you suspect a stiff scramble out. About 50 minutes from your car, the trail turns left and goes at the steep bank. For 300 feet you climb on rock steps. Deep waterbars of logs and earth prevent erosion. At the top your legs cease straining as the trail becomes less demanding. You reach another grade, which remains from the days of horse-drawn logging sleds. Spruces begin to blend with the white birches. Another steep climb brings you to a little flat where a trickle of water drips from the slope on your right.

The trail bears right to the foot of another upward pitch—again with rock steps to aid you. More important, the small boulders hold the trail in place. You may wonder at their size because they sometimes require very high lifting of your boots, with knees approaching your chin. This is not due to a wry sense of humor among trail crews. The rocks must contain enough weight to hold them in the shallow earth.

At the top of the steps you begin a steady climb. Here the trail narrows but the waterbars are adequate and the footing is good and not too rocky. The trees grow smaller. Approaching treeline? Not so. After a green tunnel 10 feet high, the larger birches reappear among tall evergreens and mountain ash trees. Look up to your right in the open woods and you'll see North Lafayette. It's not as far away as it appears.

The trail becomes typical of older routes on steep ridges. Evergreen branches reach into the narrow, rocky track and brush against your arms and hips. You grasp here and there tough roots or corners of rocks. Several short levels alternate with abrupt upward rock-scrambles, till you leave behind the final stunted spruces and stand in the open at treeline. Cairns mark the way up to the junction with the Garfield Ridge Trail.

Turn right onto the Garfield Ridge Trail. Soon you are climbing between low walls that keep you from walking on the delicate alpine vegetation. You'll see cushions of diapensia. Mountain sandwort blossoms white well into late summer when the creeping mountain cranberry has formed red fruit in the rock crevices.

The trail rises more sharply toward the sky and the scattered crags of North Lafayette. The summit is only 0.25 mile plus a few yards from the Skookumchuck Trail. It's a beautiful place for lunch—on a good day; cold winds and cloud can buffet it and smother it.

If the day is one of unlimited visibility, your luck may also bring you the thrill of watching a sailplane glide silently over your aerie.

After that, your return is an anticlimax, although pleasantly easy down the same route you climbed.

25

Cannon Mountain

Distance (round trip): 7½ miles

Walking time: 5½ hours

Vertical rise: 2100 feet

Maps: USDA/FS 7½' Franconia; USGS 7½' Franconia

You can ride in a tramway cable car to the summit, so why climb Cannon Mountain on foot? Because only your two legs can make the mountain yours. Somehow this also improves the magnificent views of Franconia Notch and Mount Lafayette. For hikers aiming to climb all 4000-footers, Cannon qualifies by 100 feet.

Skiers who have swooped down the snowy trails find that a summer climb, which pits them against this solid height unaided by tramway or T-bars, gives the mountain new meaning.

A rounded block seen from the notch, Cannon's stark cliffs loom before you as you drive north on the parkway toward the Old Man. The mountain appears as a mass of stone on which evergreens cling with minimum success. Approach from the

north, and you see its grassy ski slopes and trails like high pastures and giant paths down through the woods.

For a loop over the summit, climb the Kinsman Ridge Trail from the north and descend by the Hi-Cannon and Lonesome Lake Trails, returning through the notch to your car via the northern extension of the Pemi Trail.

Be forewarned that this is not a quiet, secluded hike. You'll be listening to the surf sound of traffic on the parkway and meeting tourists and campers.

How to Get There
On the Franconia Notch Parkway, take Exit 2 for the Cannon Mountain Tramway and Old Man Viewing. Park in the tram parking area as for Hike 23 and the Greenleaf Trail.

The asphalt covers a vanished field known as Profile Clearing. It was once the site of the immense Profile House described in Hike 19. As you leave your car, look up at the silhouette of the ridge south from the tramway. Perhaps you can discern a horizontal rock—the Cannon—aimed toward Mount Lafayette behind you and outlined against the sky. The Cannon

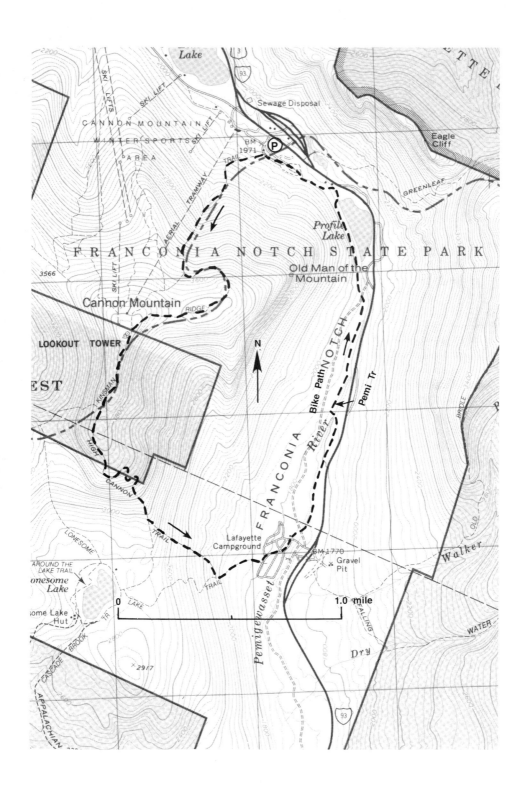

can be seen more clearly from the Old Man parking area and the Old Man viewing spot on Profile Lake.

The Trail

Your first trail for this loop hike, the Kinsman Ridge Trail, begins to the left of the tram. A Kinsman Ridge Trail sign directs you onward, 150 yards ahead. Bear right across a field below an old ski jump.

The Kinsman Ridge Trail climbs a steep bank, and at once you are on your way skyward. Steep for more than 1 mile, the trail gains altitude rapidly by a series of switchbacks. You climb to an overgrown opening in the trees and watch the cable cars slide gently up or down the black lines that suspend them.

As the trail angles away from the tramway it becomes more difficult among rock slabs, which erosion has exposed. Watch out for your footing over roots and in gullies of rotten rock Beyond this climb the trail levels out on the east shoulder. After a passage through small spruce and fir, you come to a sharp right turn. A branch trail bears left to a breathtaking view from open ledges. North and south the Franconia crests line the horizon: Eagle Cliff, Mount Lafayette, Mount Lincoln, Little Haystack, and Mount Liberty.

On a ridge several hundred yards north, and from a camouflage of evergreen scrub, the Cannon aims at Mount Lafayette. From this angle it appears in its true form—a balanced rock shelf. You may wonder whether you're on the profile's ledges. You're not. The profile is dangerous, and reinforced rocks form the brooding silhouette far down and out of sight beyond the scrub and rocks.

Return to the main Kinsman Ridge Trail. Keep past the right turn leading back the way you came. The trail crosses the east shoulder, then dips into a wooded col. Soon you make a steep climb into the open again among rock slabs and alpine vegetation. All at once you hear voices and find yourself among people at the junction with the Rim Trail from the tramway. A large sign names the peaks in the panorama. A short trail leads to the summit, and an observation tower puts you above the spruces. The tramway terminal extends out from a niche, where ski trails begin to dive down.

Joining tourists at the tower, you look down the notch and for an instant you are puzzled by a ribbon in the forest and toy cars. Across this highway, you see the Franconia Range, now part of a 360-degree view. Northward stretches the pastoral valley of the Gale River and Franconia village. South and west, a wilder panorama opens across Mount Kinsman's two summits toward Mount Moosilauke.

When you're ready to descend, return to the Kinsman Ridge Trail. Follow it where it passes southward below the summit from the junction where you turned up to the tower. (The trail continues its rugged way 15 miles to its southern end at the Lost River Road in Kinsman Notch.) Follow it only about 0.5 mile to the Hi-Cannon Trail where you turn left for the descent.

The Hi-Cannon Trail takes you past a lookoff ledge opening toward Mount Kinsman on your right and Lonesome Lake below you. The trail swings through firs above cliffs from which there are wide outlooks into the notch with its parallel ranges east and west. You climb down rocks on a ladder and pass the eave-like ledges called Cliff House on your left.

Continue down a rough stretch into less precipitous woods. Keep left past

the Dodge Cutoff which leads to Lonesome Lake. Hi-Cannon's switchbacks take you down to the Lonesome Lake Trail. Turn left and walk this graded path to the Lafayette Campground. Follow yellow blazes through the campground to a Pemi Trail sign, which faces away from you, just before a footbridge. Turn left on the Pemi Trail. It crosses the main entrance road before a bridge; look for the Pemi Trail sign, TO VIEW POINT OF OLD MAN.

Or you may want to walk the bike path, which you'll find to the left of a log cabin. The Pemi Trail follows the stream, mostly on the route of the former Profile Lake Trail, and provides more real woodsy footing. Both routes take you to Profile Lake in about 2 miles. Here the Pemi Trail bears left along the west shore of the lake, whereas the bike path curves north under the parkway, then back toward the lakeside viewing area for the Old Man. Either way you will be joining tourists and sightseers for your return to your car.

Winter view from Cannon Mountain

26

Mount Kinsman

Distance (round trip): 10 miles

Walking time: 8 hours

Vertical rise: 3400 feet

*Maps: USDA/FS 7½' Sugar Hill;
USGS 7½' Sugar Hill; USDA/FS 7½'
Franconia; USGS 7½' Franconia;
USDA/FS 7½' Lincoln; USGS 7½'
Lincoln*

Mount Kinsman has two summits. A
wooded col and 1 mile of the Kinsman Ridge Trail connect them. The
mountain forms a divide that separates the Merrimack River tributaries
from the Connecticut River watershed
to the west.

The north peak, elevation 4293 feet,
drops away 500 feet to narrow Kinsman Pond and the roof of the shelter
near the spruce-grown shore. Beyond
to the east, Lonesome Lake sparkles
in the evergreen forest above Franconia Notch. Mount Lafayette, the giant of the region, rises across the notch.

The south peak's dome, elevation
4358 feet, because of topography and
exposure, extends into the alpine-

tundra zone above treeline, and provides views in all directions. From both
summits, the Franconia Range out-
lines the eastern horizon. Sun and
clouds endlessly shift lighting effects
across the slopes.

Although hikers most often climb
Mount Kinsman from Lonesome Lake,
the route described here has the advantage of being less traveled and quite
removed from the popularity of the
Franconia Notch area. This hike takes
you over both peaks and returns you
by the same route. The Mount Kinsman Trail begins from the west in
Easton, a township now grown back
to woods from family farms of the 19th
century. The Mount Kinsman Trail
climbs to the Kinsman Ridge Trail,
which traverses both summits.

Easton's settlement began at the
conclusion of the Revolution. About
1783, Nathan Kinsman cut the first
narrow woods-track into the wilderness territory that is now Easton. He
brought in tools and supplies on six
mules. He built a log cabin on his
grant of 600 acres. More settlers fol-
lowed.

As in other mountain towns, the
small meadows of Easton's valley and
its rocky pastures fed and clothed an

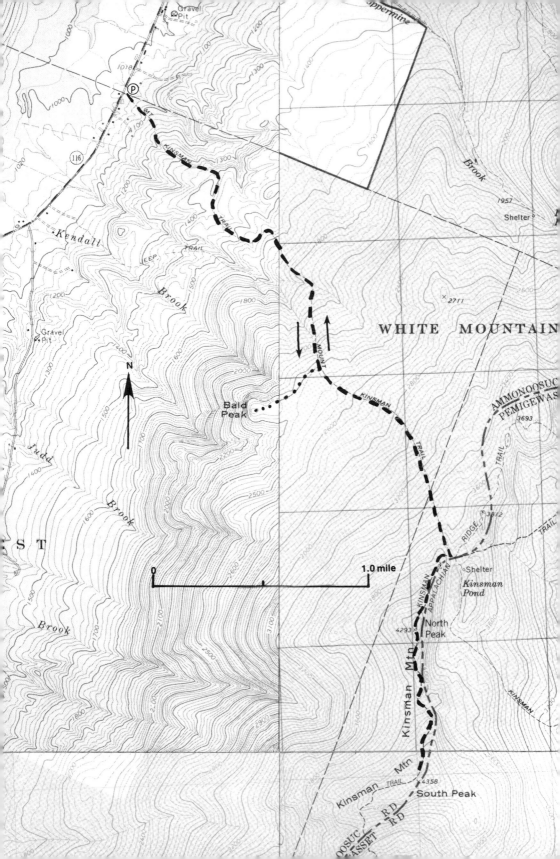

Gravel
Pit

P

116

Kendall

Gravel
Pit

Judd
Brook

KINSMAN

TRAIL

JEEP   TRAIL

Brook

N

Bald
Peak

Coppermine

Brook

1957
Shelter

2711

WHITE MOUNTAIN

MOUNT

KINSMAN

AMMONOOSUC
PEMIGEWAS
3693

TRAIL

3812

Kinsman
Pond

Shelter

RIDGE

TRAIL

Kinsman Mtn

KINSMAN

APPALACHIAN

4293

North
Peak

KINSMAN

1.0 mile

0

Brook

Kinsman Mtn TRAIL

4358   South Peak

OOSUC RD

ASSET   RD

increasing population for 75 years until the Civil War. Then war casualties, hopes of easier western land, and cash wages from city industry drained away the young men. Now along NH 116, trees grow tall in the old farmland. The Mount Kinsman Trail crosses through some of this earlier farmland as it approaches the mountain's broad west slope.

How to Get There
The trail begins on the east side of NH 116, 7 miles north of Bungay Corner (on NH 112 west of Kinsman Notch). From the village of Franconia, the trail is 4 miles south on NH 116. Watch the mileage and go slowly or you'll miss the entrance road. It's identified by the highway's town line marker for Easton and Franconia. A gate and two large gateposts of laid-up stone bar the entrance to vehicles. Parking can be off to one side of the gate or along the highway shoulder.

The Trail
The trail follows a bulldozed logging road through sandy cuts. It is bordered by spruces and birches in the old pastures. The road becomes a wide path through a stand of maples near a sugar house.

Climbing more steeply, you approach a brook after 1.5 miles. Cross the brook, bearing right, and climb up a steeper logging road. You will soon step over another brook with a mossy ledge on the left, then Flume Brook. A branch trail leads down to a ravine and cascade. Shortly beyond Flume Brook, the main trail turns sharply left. A branch trail to the right leads to Bald Peak 0.25 mile through woods to wide views from rocks and blueberry bushes.

The main trail follows the dwindling brook. You look up at the steep ridge ahead. The trail rises steadily through spruces and firs. Golden-crowned kinglets, feeding in the upper branches, give notice of their presence only by faint cheeping notes and by small flutterings. But, if you look behind you on the steeper pitches, you can see the tiny birds in the tree-tops level with your eyes.

Among stunted evergreens you reach the Kinsman Ridge Trail. (This trail is a long, 16-mile trek over Cannon Mountain and Mount Kinsman to Kinsman Notch.) Turn right, south, on the Kinsman Ridge Trail. Take note of this junction so you'll recognize it on your return. The Kinsman Ridge Trail, along here, makes a narrow passage through evergreens and leads over rocky ledges to the north peak.

The north summit is partially wooded yet it offers a sudden view of Mount Lafayette, which becomes breathtaking from the cliff reached by a short trail left, east, down among rocks and spruces. The jagged Franconia Range cuts across the eastern horizon.

To continue, climb back up the spur trail to the Kinsman Ridge Trail. Turn left and continue south. You descend to the col and climb up out of the evergreens to the bare south dome and the summit cairn. On several acres of open rock and dwarf spruces trimmed by the wind, you wander among abundant mountain plants, lichens, mosses, sedges, and grasses. In places, a matted turf has formed, held down by the roots of dwarf blueberry, Labrador tea, and mountain cranberry. Cool breezes and fine views make this the hike's ideal lunch setting.

In the afternoon, go back north along the Kinsman Ridge Trail over the north peak. Watch for the left turn into the Mount Kinsman Trail. Follow the route of your ascent, and remember not to be fooled at the corner where the Bald Peak spur trail invites you straight ahead; turn sharply right, down the straight logging road, then bear left across the brook.

27

Mount Moosilauke

Distance (round trip): 6¾ miles

Walking time: 6 hours

Vertical rise: 2400 feet

Maps: USDA/FS 7½' Mt. Kineo; USGS 7½' Mt. Kineo; USDA/FS 7½' Mt. Moosilauke; USGS 7½' Mt. Moosilauke

Rise early for Mount Moosilauke. It's a destination and an event. Bulking large on the southwestern border of the mountains, elevation 4802 feet, massive and alone, its bare summit commands wide views in a complete circle.

The Franconias, 14 miles northeast, march across the horizon. Far beyond them, Mount Washington appears with other Presidential peaks. More to the east, Mount Carrigain stands sentinel at the eastern approach to the Pemigewasset Wilderness, which is bordered on the south by Mounts Hancock, Osceola, Tripyramid, and the Sandwich Range. Directly south, smaller mountains scattered in the foothills blend toward isolated Mount Kearsarge (South) and Mount Cardigan. Westward, across the verdant Connecticut River valley, Vermont's Green Mountains extend as far as Killington Peak, Mount Mansfield, and Jay Peak.

Mount Moosilauke has been popular for more than a hundred years. In 1860, Sam Holt built his stone Prospect House on the windswept summit. The opening ceremonies on the Fourth of July, according to one authority, attracted a thousand men and women. The gala crowd included a brass band, orators, militia, and Native Americans. Refreshments were served. The Carriage Road continued to bring guests from Warren.

The Carriage Road was still safe for horse-drawn rigs in 1917. Dartmouth College took over the hotel in 1920 and put in bunks and accommodations for 80 hikers. In the summer, students managed the Summit House, or Tip Top House as it was then called. Moosilauke has remained Dartmouth's mountain, although the Summit House burned in 1942. For a number of years the Dartmouth Outing Club maintained an emergency cabin below the summit, but by 1978 overuse and vandalism made its removal necessary.

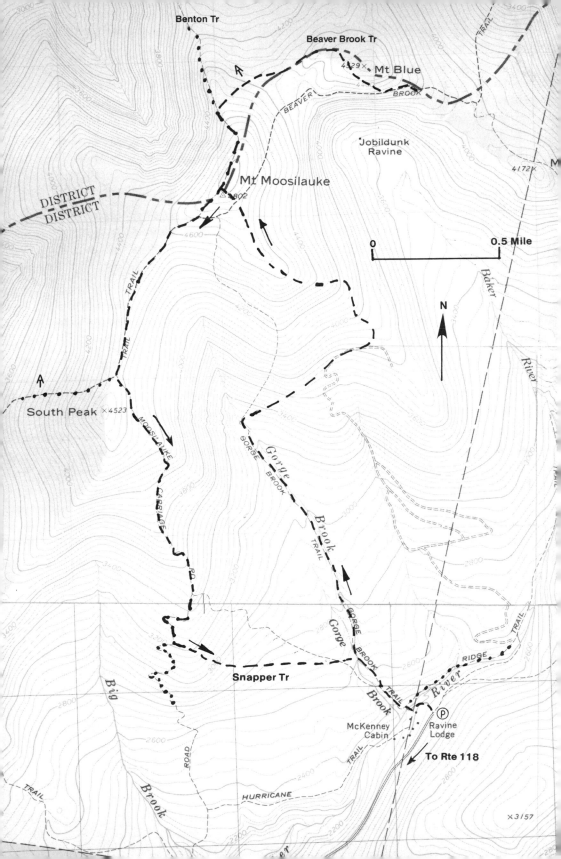

The college land is managed as a wilderness area where overnight camping and open fires are not permitted. This policy of limited use is designed to protect the unique and fragile mountain environment.

At all times the mountain can be cold and icy. Gales sweep down upon it with dangerous speed and intensity. Above treeline, clouds often shroud the rocks. The south shoulder, 1 mile long, is exposed to storms, and on a gloomy day suggests the beginning of the world despite the trail along the old Carriage Road traversing its length.

How to Get There

The trails starting near Dartmouth's Ravine Lodge offer the widest selection and most spectacular routes. Turn west off NH 118 between Warren and North Woodstock, 6 miles from Warren, onto the access road to the lodge. Drive 1.5 miles to a turnaround. Head back along the road and park on the right-hand shoulder.

The Trail

With adequate clothing for this above-treeline climb, and, of course, food and water, walk to the left side of the turnaround, northwest, near a sign for ALL TRAILS. Take the path down to the Baker River—here a large brook. Turn right over the footbridge. On the west bank, the Gorge Brook Trail begins to your left. (To the right, the Asquam-Ridge Trail leads upstream for a much longer route to the summit via the Beaver Brook Trail.)

Take the path left along the bank. The trail swings right, and you begin the climb. After 0.25 mile the Snapper Trail branches left. (In combination with a section of the Carriage Road, it will be your return route.)

The Gorge Brook Trail rises steadily, following an old logging road through mixed growths of hardwoods and spruces beside Gorge Brook's pools and cascades.

After the second crossing of the brook, you'll find yourself on the new trail, which avoids the eroded and steeper former ascent. This new route was completed by Put Blodgett of the Dartmouth Outing Club in 1990. Views are cleared. At 2.3 miles you'll reach an outlook with Mount Carr in the foreground, Mount Cardigan to the right, and Mount Kearsarge to the left. At 2.9 miles there are two views, the first eastward to the southern White Mountains, the second northeast over Jobildunc Ravine and Mounts Jim and Waternomee to Mount Lafayette and other White Mountain peaks.

At about 3.1 miles the trail swings left at a rock staircase and begins what is called the "Balcony" section—a traverse across the east shoulder, with wide views southeast and southwest.

As you near treeline, signs warn of the fragile alpine vegetation and ask you to stay on the trail.

Scrubby heaths alternate with twisted evergreens. The trail, marked by cairns up the treeless alpine sward and ledges, continues to the rocky summit, to the rectangular stone foundations that once supported the Summit House, and to the encompassing panorama.

For your descent, take the Carriage Road south along the rocky ridge. (If a storm threatens while you are on the summit, return by the Gorge Brook Trail.) The Dartmouth Outdoors Programs Office and the US Forest Service have completed the reconstruction of the Carriage Road, to limit erosion, provide emergency access, and make the trail more usable.

About 1 mile south of the summit on the Carriage Road, the Glencliff Trail, a link in the route the Appalachian Trail follows to Hanover and on into Vermont, drops down into the woods, right. A short way along the Glencliff Trail, a spur leads 0.2 mile west to the South Peak for a view of the forested Baker River Valley, Lake Tarleton, Mount Cube, Smarts Mountain, and various ponds.

Continue down the Carriage Road about 1.25 miles farther to the Snapper Trail, where you turn left. This former downhill racing ski trail is now a gentle grade. The loop is completed down at Gorge Brook Trail, about 1 mile.

28

Mount Garfield

Distance (round trip): 9½ miles

Walking time: 5½ hours

Vertical rise: 3100 feet

Maps: USDA/FS 7½' Franconia; USGS 7½' Franconia; USDA/FS 7½' South Twin Mtn.; USGS 7½' South Twin Mtn.

Mount Garfield's rocky summit commands a spectacular and unique view across a northern valley of the Pemigewasset Wilderness. Due south from Mount Garfield, Owl's Head—itself a 4025-foot mountain—blocks the valley and forces Franconia Brook east, while forming a narrow gap below the Franconia Range. There, on the west, Mounts Lafayette and Lincoln rise to a heavy, peaked ridge. Mount Liberty stands alone, and Flume's spire farther south has its separate identity.

You look east down to the AMC's Garfield Ridge Campsite and Shelter. Away off in that direction, Galehead Hut appears as a toy building among miles of evergreens. A line of summits shapes the eastern horizon and extends southward from North Twin over South Twin, Zealand Mountain, Guyot, and Bond to Bondcliff in the Pemigewasset River's East Branch valley.

The Garfield Trail approaches the mountain from US 3 and takes you up the long western slope to the steep cone, at 4500 feet.

How to Get There
Drive north through Franconia Notch on the parkway. As this scenic route again becomes I-93, turn right onto US 3 and follow it for 5 miles toward Twin Mountain. At a hiker sign and a sign for the Gale River Trail, turn right onto the Gale River Loop Road. Drive about 3 miles, past the trailhead for the Gale River Trail, to the Garfield Trail sign and parking on the left.

The Trail
The Garfield Trail is one of the pleasantest trails in the mountains. It begins at an embankment, keeps to a low ridge, and crosses Thompson Brook and Spruce Brook. At an intersection with the Heritage Trail, which is also a snowmobile trail with bridges spanning the brooks, use care to stay

on the Garfield Trail uphill.

Your boots and legs find easy walking on this old tractor road that served the old summit tower. The grades are fine for steady walking. You continue past trees that form a protected corridor between area logged in the early 1970s, now an interesting example of thickly sprouting growth after clearcuts. Forest renewal can be compared because the trees along the trail grew after the forest fire of 1902. For years the trail traversed burned country. As often happens after forest fires, birches took over the scorched land. Their snowy trunks with the black splashes now shine in sunlight along your way.

After a short downhill grade below a ledgy bank, left, the trail climbs the steeper slope by long inclines between switchback turns. The birches yield to spruce/fir woods higher up. The trail steepens as it bears east. The evergreens become smaller, with gnarled birch and mountain ash interspersed beside the rocky outcrops and stone steps that now often form the trail.

Climbing around a corner to the right, you head south to join the Garfield Ridge Trail for the summit approach. (This trail comes up on the left from the Garfield Ridge Campsite.) The two trails ascend as one for a scramble of less than 0.25 mile up the final pitch. The trail suggests a crude rock stairway between low spruces, which offer handholds.

At the crest, turn left. It's 50 yards to the summit rocks and a former tower's concrete foundation. (Garfield Ridge Trail continues to Mount Lafayette.)

In August 1907, Mount Garfield overlooked a holocaust. Twenty-five thousand acres, left in slash by the lumber king, J.E. ("Ave") Henry, burst into flame as lightning struck the east

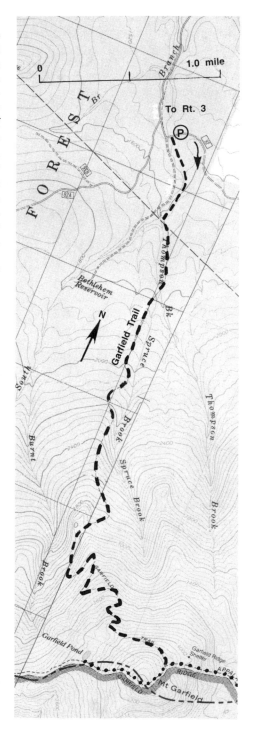

side of Owl's Head. This fire was one of many that brought militant attention to the desolation caused by lumbermen, and led to the Weeks Act of 1911 that established the White Mountain National Forest.

Old loggers, who chopped trees and earned a hard living in the forests they devastated, used to look back with nostalgia and tell yarns about J.E. Henry, who hired them and made a fortune. Henry, a once-barefoot poor boy, became legendary for his toughness, determination, and parsimony. The territory he clear-cut often went up in terrible forest fires.

There's no loop to this hike. Return by the same route you came.

29

Mount Osceola

Distance (Tripoli Road to main peak and return): 6½ miles

Walking time: 4½ hours

Vertical rise: 2025 feet

Maps: USDA/FS 7½' Waterville Valley; USGS 7½' Waterville Valley; USDA/FS 7½' Mt. Osceola; USGS 7½' Mt. Osceola

Tripoli Road, Breadtray Ridge, Thornton Gap, Scar Ridge, Mad River—these colorful names from loggers' parlance enliven maps of the country that surrounds this peak named for the famous Seminole warrior. Mount Osceola dominates the upper end of Waterville Valley. Its 4340-foot elevation viewed from the west appears as a single summit, but, seen from the east along the Kancamagus Highway, the East Peak's 4156-foot shoulder enlarges the mountain.

How to Get There

The most direct trail to the main summit begins at Waterville Valley's north-west pass, Thornton Gap. From Campton, drive east on NH 49, 10 miles up the Mad River. Turn left, and drive past the access road to Tecumseh Ski Area. This Tripoli Road crests 4.5 miles from NH 49 at the 2300-foot pass. About 200 yards beyond, the Mount Osceola Trail enters the woods on the right (north), where there is a parking area.

If you are coming from I-93, Exit 31, drive the Tripoli Road 7 miles to the parking area, on the left.

The Trail

At the start of the Mount Osceola Trail, you climb a stony section, but the grade is comfortable as the trail becomes a series of gravel switchbacks. More switchbacks take you up Breadtray Ridge. Most of the views along the way are overgrown, but there is a fine one of Mount Tecumseh's ski trails and Sandwich Mountain to the south beyond the green Waterville Valley. You cross a little brook on stepping stones. The trail swings right and left several times, and you walk through muddy patches, across moss-bordered ledges. Near the top of the ridge, the trail turns sharply right, east, and leads

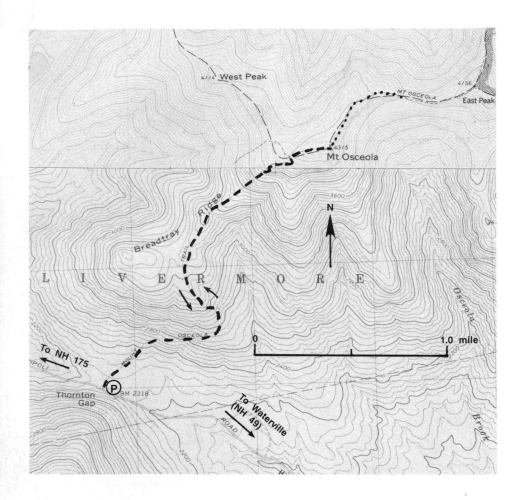

up to the level approach through summit spruces to the ledges and the sites of two former fire towers.

At the first site, where the older tower stood, take the path to the left for the view to the north. Then continue on to the site of the second tower and the extensive view from the ledges. Scrub spruce obscures some of the outlook.

You are now standing on the highest of the mountains encircling Waterville Valley. The panorama off this isolated summit shows the following in the direction listed: Slightly south of east, Mount Tripyramid's three peaks notch the horizon 5 miles away. An unusual nearby view extends north into the valley along Hancock Branch and the Kancamagus Highway. On the right of Mount Hancock, and more distant, Mount Carrigain's angular bulk gives you a line on Mount Washington, 22 miles away. Turning northwest, you can orient yourself by the sentinel, Mount Garfield, and find to your left Mounts Lafayette and Lincoln. Of the remaining Franconias, Mounts Liberty and

On Mount Osceola

Flume are pinnacles in the direction of Cannon Mountain. More to the west, Kinsman's north and south summits appear as a ridge, but Mount Moosilauke stands out as the important western peak.

Return to the Tripoli Road by the route of ascent.

Those hardy souls who yearn to climb all the accepted 4000-foot peaks will continue east on the Mount Osceola Trail, and will think nothing of the descent and climb to East Peak 1 mile away. They may even keep on down the steep and hazardous trail to Greeley Ponds and out to the Kancamagus Highway for a total of 7 miles from the Tripoli Road. (See Hike 7.) Or you may walk from Mad River Notch in the opposite direction past Greeley Ponds to Waterville Valley at Depot Camp. For either of these exploits allow 3 hours more than Osceola alone, and arrange for transportation at the end.

30

Mount Tripyramid

Distance (round trip): 11 miles

Walking time: 7 hours

Vertical rise (including all three peaks): 3050 feet

Maps: USDA/FS 7½' Mt. Tripyramid; USGS 15' Mt. Chocorua; USDA/FS 7½' Waterville Valley; USGS 7½' Waterville Valley

The name describes the three peaks; it says nothing about the two slides. For pure joy in climbing, the North Slide is hard to beat. You choose your own way over the angular ledges. There is little danger in dry weather. A wild and extensive view opens behind you.

From the Livermore Road out of Waterville Valley, you hike a loop up the exciting North Slide, over the three peaks, down the treacherous South Slide, and back to the road. The slides tore out the woods and rocks on both North and South Peaks in 1885. The slides are completely unlike, the North Slide being ledges, the South Slide rocks and gravel. The three peaks rise in a line from a ridge about 1 mile

long. North Peak's elevation is 4140 feet. Middle Peak reaches to 4110 feet. South Peak crests at 4090 feet.

How to Get There

From Campton, drive east on NH 49, 10 miles up the Mad River. Turn left onto the Tripoli Road and drive past the access road to Tecumseh Ski Area. At 1.8 miles from NH 49, turn right across the Mad River's West Branch. Just beyond the bridge, turn sharp left at a gate into the parking area. The road to the right continues on to Waterville village.

The Trail

The hike begins at a kiosk at the east end of the parking area. Turn onto the Livermore Road. This shaded gravel road is also the Livermore Trail. Keep past the Greeley Ponds Trail on your left. You soon cross a bridge over the Mad River.

You'll pass other trails that are part of the hiking and ski touring system maintained by the Waterville Valley Athletic and Improvement Association. At 2.1 miles Cascade Path bears right across Avalanche Brook on a creosoted, heavy-timbered bridge. Don't take it. Stay on your side of the

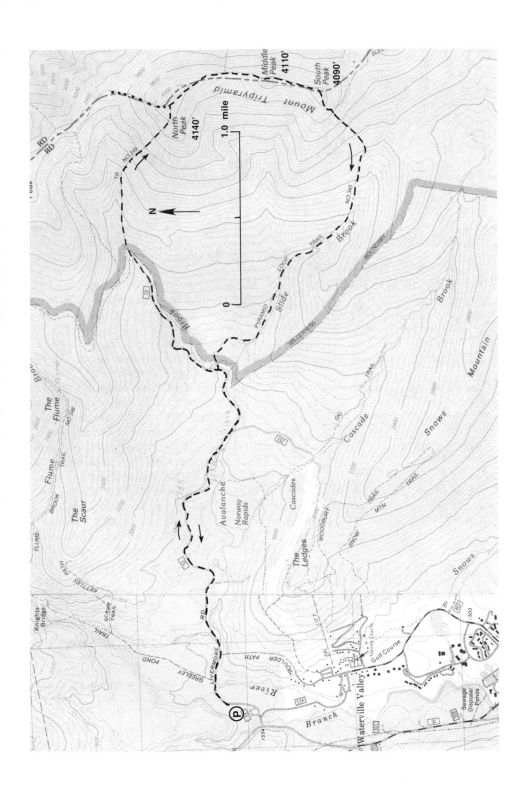

brook, the north or left bank, on the Livermore Road.

This will bring you to the trail on the right for Tripyramid's South Slide. It is your return route after you climb over the mountain's three summits. Another 0.5 mile and you pass through the opening that was once Avalanche Camp back during the ax-crosscut-saw era in the White Mountains. You are approaching the start of the climb— it's 0.5 mile farther. Watch for a hairpin turn to the left. The Mount Tripyramid Trail to the North Slide drops off the road to your right at the corner. (The Livermore Road continues and becomes a hikers' trail over Livermore Pass and down to the Kancamagus Highway 4 miles north.)

(*Note:* The Slide is dangerous when wet or icy. For a trail that bypasses it, proceed up the Livermore Road 0.25 mile and turn right onto the Scaur Ridge Trail. This trail loops eastward toward Scaur Peak and a ridge connecting with North Tripyramid, where it joins the Pine Bend Brook Trail coming up from the Kancamagus Highway to the North Peak. This safer route is only about 0.75 mile longer than via the North Slide.)

On a dry, warm day, climb down from the hairpin turn and cross Avalanche Brook. Climb the bank beyond the brook and follow the trail upstream, left, for a 0.5-mile walk on this former logging road to the base of the slide.

The yellow blazes on the rocks are faded and difficult to see. Take time to look for them—and to turn and admire the view behind you. If you wander off, just remember to bear

right near the top. You'll see two large cairns there. The trail enters the spruces at the upper left corner.

The short remaining climb in the woods takes you to the North Peak. The tremendous 180-degree view is now overgrown, but look for glimpses of the Franconia Range and Mount Washington—all from a rare angle across the Kancamagus Highway and over the forests of the Pemigewasset Wilderness.

The Pine Bend Brook Trail joins the Mount Tripyramid Trail to become the route south down the ridge. The Pine Bend Brook Trail ends after 0.5 mile at the Sabbaday Brook Trail, left (from the Kancamagus Highway). You keep straight along and begin the climb up Middle Peak. There's a good view west from a ledge near the summit of Middle Peak. Continue on to South Peak.

Descending, you come to the South Slide and to forested vistas stretching away west. The two Flat Mountain Ponds lie in a hollow left of Sandwich Mountain. Ski trails identify Mount Tecumseh. Mount Moosilauke dominates the western horizon.

About 60 yards down the slide, the Sleeper Trail comes in on your left from Mount Whiteface. Keep on down the slide. Watch for rolling gravel and loose rocks as you place your feet. At the base of the slide, bear right. The trail enters the woods, crosses several small brooks, then makes a crossing over Avalanche Brook to the terminus at Livermore Road. Turn left down the road for the return to your car.

31

Between the Notches: Zeacliff

*Distance (round trip via Twinway):
7½ miles; (round trip, including loop
through Zealand Notch): 9¼ miles*

*Walking time (via Twinway): 4½
hours; (through Zealand Notch):6½
hours*

Vertical rise: 1500 feet

*Maps: USDA/FS 7½' Crawford
Notch; USGS 7½' Crawford Notch*

The roadless upper watershed of the
Pemigewasset River's East Branch sepa-
rates Franconia Notch and Crawford
Notch and their adjacent mountains.
Part of this is now the Pemigewasset
Wilderness. Long known as the "Pemi
Wilderness," it has become an offi-
cially designated Wilderness by act of
Congress. The main highways circle
this country and leave the tourist
unaware of the forested valleys and
peaks between the two sections of the
White Mountains. A hike to Zeacliff
fills this vacancy.

You approach this great outlook
along an abandoned railroad grade
once used to haul logs out to the mills.
The grade parallels the Zealand River
toward its source. Beavers dam the
branching streams. Zealand Pond, at
the end of swampy meadows, has two
outlets. Mid-June is a fine time to walk
the Zealand Trail and look for birds.
At that time, too, the rhodora blooms
pink across the bogs.

Perched above the pond, the AMC's
Zealand Falls Hut offers accommodations to 36 hikers and a view directly
to Mount Carrigain.

Zeacliff is about 1.5 miles above by
the Twinway, a mountain trail. This
steady climb brings you to Zeacliff's
lookoff ledge above wooded valleys
and mountains stretching away south
and east, with views of Zealand Notch
and Whitewall Mountain, both seared
by fire during and after the logging
days of the 1880s and early 1900s. This
old, slashed and burned country has
grown up largely to hardwoods. Former
logging roads appear as green ribbons along distant contours of lighter
growth. Sometimes ravens hover over
the cliffs.

How to Get There
To reach the beginning of the Zealand
Trail and the railroad grade, drive to

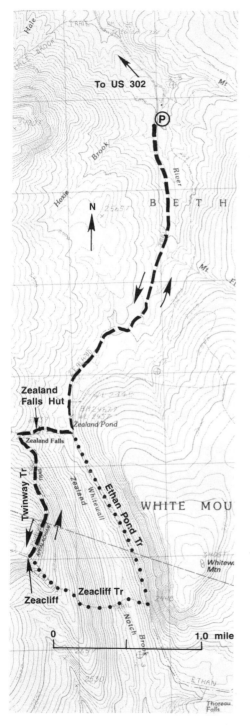

the Zealand Campground on US 302, 2.5 miles east from Twin Mountain village. Turn south on the forest service's Zealand Road, which crosses the Ammonoosuc River and leads up a steep hill to a steadily ascending valley. Pass the Sugarloaf Camping Areas and continue to the Zealand Road's end, 3.5 miles from the highway.

The Trail

Walk to the south end of the parking area, where there are signs. The Zealand Trail follows the railroad grade except for short sections cut through the woods where the railroad once crossed the Zealand River for short distances. In this way the trail keeps west of the dwindling river, which divides into its source streams. You approach Zealand Pond through a boggy country of meadows and beaver ponds.

This open country has varying water levels due to the beavers and to their instinct to dam all running water. You'll find that most of the brooks have footbridges and that the wooden walkways help keep your feet dry. The plants and birds in this habitat include the tiny insectivorous sundew clinging to a rotten log half-submerged in water. High on a dead stub, the sturdy olive-sided flycatcher calls out stridently "*hic-three-beers.*" During May the shadbushes, one species of which can grow to 20 feet, bloom in white splendor. Sections of the old railroad grade are visible above the bogs.

At 2.25 miles from the start of the Zealand Trail, the A-Z Trail enters from the left. (The A-Z Trail connects to trails from the Crawford House site and Crawford Notch's Willey Range.) You cross the north outlet of Zealand Pond and follow the east shore. At the south end, where you make a sharp right turn, the Ethan Pond Trail en-

ters from the left. (The Ethan Pond Trail leads through Zealand Notch.) Keep right, across a wet section at the south outlet of Zealand Pond. Soon you climb the trail's only steep rise to its terminus at the Zealand Falls Hut, 2700 feet elevation. (The AMC keeps the hut open in winter on a caretaker basis. Cross-country skiing on plenty of good snow makes this region of special interest.)

Behind the hut, take the Twinway Trail up past the Lend-a-Hand Trail at the right. (The Lend-a-Hand Trail climbs Mount Hale.) Cross the small Whitewall Brook above the falls. The Twinway Trail is rough and steep compared to the previous railroad grade. White birches grow smaller as the trail climbs into stunted spruces. It emerges on the rocky summit of the ridge leading toward Zealand Mountain, Mount Guyot, and South Twin. At a view sign just before the summit rocks, bear left for the top of Zeacliff, which is on a short loop off the Twinway Trail. The cliff overlooks Zealand Notch and faces Whitewall Mountain.

You are looking across the eastern area of the Pemigewasset Wilderness and the Lincoln Woods Scenic Area, thousands of acres preserved in their wildness. Mount Carrigain towers over the forest, a spruce-clad pyramid topped by an observation platform. Ponds draining into the Pemigewasset River's East Branch glisten in the valleys. To the left of Carrigain you sight through Carrigain Notch next to Mount Lowell. To the right of Carrigain, Mount Hancock is a solid outline. Closer and to the west, Mount Bond reaches away south from its barren crown.

If you are in shape for a tough and dramatic descent, your return need not be back to the hut the way you came. Fair warning: this loop is not for picnickers. If you decide you're rugged enough, walk west along the Twinway almost 0.25 mile and turn left onto the Zeacliff Trail. It at once drops off the side of the mountain into evergreen forest with eroded roots, rocks, and bare rock faces sometimes more than 10 feet high. You descend into a forest of white birches along a southerly ridge, then drop again in a series of steep pitches between level little plateaus. Through the leaves you may catch glimpses of the slides and cliffs of Whitewall Mountain across Zealand Notch.

You reach the bottom of the ridge at a stretch of spruce and balsam woods before you come to the alders along Whitewall Brook. It's a tidy little stream, and you can cross on rocks, usually. Beyond it you climb a wooded slide into the open of barren rock slabs and jagged talus. The formations suggest an abandoned quarry. Follow blue blazes up the rock-scramble to the Ethan Pond Trail. Turn left, north, for the hike back to Zealand Pond along the old railroad grade. This loop is a distance of 3 miles as compared to the 1.5 miles back the way you came from Zealand Falls Hut. But it's an experience passing through Zealand Notch before hiking out to your car.

View from Zeacliff

MOUNT WASHINGTON REGION

And that night in the log cave, on the fragrant boughs, I listened to the wind outside and I was snug in a mountain fastness and knew the feeling that went with the strange word: fastness. Peaks out there in the darkness. Mount Washington, Jefferson, Adams, Madison.

—Daniel Doan
Our Last Backpack

32

Pinkham Notch: The Crew-Cut Trail

Distance (round trip): 1¾ miles

Walking time: 1¼ hours

Vertical rise: 400 feet

Maps: USDA/FS 7½' Mt. Washington SE; USGS 7½' x 15' Mt. Washington; USDA/FS 7½' Carter Dome; USGS 7½' Carter Dome

Pinkham Notch appears less spectacular near the highway than either Franconia or Crawford Notch. But, situated close under Mount Washington's eastern ravines, Pinkham Notch has its own distinction: it's a climbing center. It's as near as you can drive on a main highway (NH 16) to the most impressive mountain in New England—Mount Washington. Major trails pass through or start in Pinkham Notch. It's the mountain climbers' base, a takeoff for the Presidential Range.

Pinkham Notch has changed since 1826, when Daniel Pinkham built the road through his grant between Jackson and Randolph. Now there's the wide highway: traffic on NH 16 would astound Daniel Pinkham. The AMC's Pinkham Notch Visitor Center (10 miles north of Jackson), established in 1920, has outgrown the original log cabins and has become a complex, modern headquarters for the AMC's Huts and Trail System, with plentiful parking and accommodations for 100 guests. At Wildcat Ski Area the gondola lift operates year-round.

As part of an introductory hike, the 1-mile Crew-Cut Trail winds through hardwood forest to a lookout ledge at the north end of Pinkham Notch.

How to Get There
To start the hike, turn west off NH 16 at Pinkham Notch Visitor Center. Leave your car in the parking area.

The Trail
Walk past the lodge toward Mount Washington. Turn right to the Tuckerman Ravine Trail. About 300 feet past the buildings on the right, watch for the sign to the Old Jackson Road. Bear right on this trail. Cross a work road,

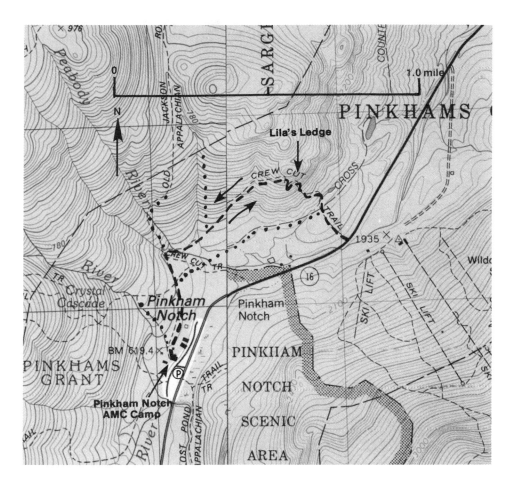

following the white blazes on trees. The trail winds through open woods about 0.25 mile to a junction where the Blanchard and Connie's Way ski trails cross it. Continue on the Old Jackson Road. Immediately after a wooden bridge, the Crew-Cut Trail branches right.

Follow the blue blazes across a seasonal brook and on through beech and yellow birch trees. Across the second brook, keep straight past the George's Gorge Trail, left. Continue following the blue blazes. The trail climbs over a knoll and enters an area of broken ledges under the tall trees as it approaches the base of a cliff. The main trail goes straight. A spur trail to the left leads to the lookout called Lila's Ledge. This pinnacle offers a view from its lower corner toward Wildcat Ski Area. Above, for the experienced and agile climber, a wide view opens into Pinkham Notch and up to Mount Washington.

The main trail, avoiding the cliff, curves left and goes down steeply across several levels of the slope. It passes through the seepage from a small bog shortly before reaching NH 16, 50

An autumn hike

yards south and opposite the ski area's parking lot.

Return to your car by the same route you came.

33

Lowe's Bald Spot

Distance (round trip): 4¼ miles

Walking time: 2¾ hours

Vertical rise: 1000 feet

Maps: USDA/FS 7½' Mt. Washington SE; USGS 7½' x 15' Mt. Washington

The half-day excursion from Pinkham Notch to Lowe's Bald Spot takes you to a 3000-foot opening on Mount Washington's eastern slope. By easy trails you experience the mountain's sweep and primitive power. You look away to the peaks north and west. Wide views open east to the Carter Range and south through Pinkham Notch. Lowe's Bald Spot gives you mountain air and sunlight, distant skies, and the near scent of fir balsam.

How to Get There

Turn off NH 16 for parking at the AMC's Pinkham Notch Visitor Center.

The Trail

Beyond the lodge take the Tuckerman Ravine Trail for about 300 feet to the sign for the Old Jackson Road, right. The Old Jackson Road is part of the AT and thus has white blazes; it was once a route for horse-drawn vehicles from Pinkham Notch to the carriage road, now the auto road. Follow the white blazes straight across a junction with the Blanchard and Connie's Way ski trails at about 0.25 mile. You cross a wooden bridge at about 0.5 mile. Here the Crew Cut Trail branches right. Keep straight up the hill ahead. After crossing two brooks, you see George's Gorge Trail come in on your right at about 1 mile. Continue on the Old Jackson Road, over several brooks, to a sharp left turn onto a 1977 trail cut to avoid a section of the auto road. The trail rises steeply on

Warning sign, Mount Washington

FRED BAVENDAM

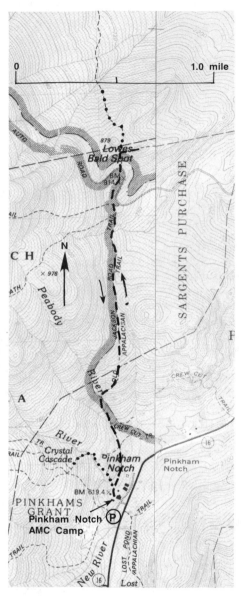

rock steps before leveling somewhat and passing the Raymond Path at 1.7 mile, to your left, and then the Nelson Crag Trail, also left. (See Hike 37, The Alpine Garden.) By now, you'll be hearing vehicles on the auto road. Climb onward to an old gravel pit, which the trail crosses. You come out on the auto road above the 2-mile marker. On the other side of the road, take the Madison Gulf Trail. You are continuing on the AT as it enters the Great Gulf Wilderness.

Follow the Madison Gulf Trail 0.25 mile to a branch trail, right, and the short climb to Lowe's Bald Spot. (The Madison Gulf Trail continues to the Great Gulf, up to treeline, and to the AMC's Madison Hut in the barren col between Mount Adams and Mount Madison, the northeastern pinnacle of the Presidential Range. The trail is also a link to the Great Gulf Trail and the trails leaving the Gulf for the high peaks. The entire Madison Gulf Trail takes 5 hours of steady hiking and strenuous climbing up the steep headwall of Madison Gulf.)

After the short climb from the main trail, you cross two ledges before getting to the highest, Lowe's Bald Spot. Look north across the lower valley of the Great Gulf and the West Branch of the Peabody River to Mount Adams and Mount Madison. West is the headwall of Huntington Ravine topped by Nelson Crag and the bare cone of Mount Washington, a desert of jumbled stones rising in unforgettable contrast to the green trees below. Up there, earth's verdure emerges miraculously from its mineral source. Yet the grim environment might suggest to you an atomic blast's rubble. If it does, you are happy to hear the birds singing in the nearby spruces and to see hikers on the trails, and almost relieved to hear autos grinding up the road.

34

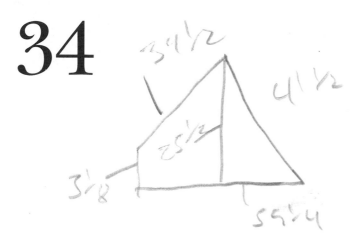

Glen Boulder

Distance (to Glen Boulder and back):
3 miles

Walking time: 3½ hours

Vertical rise: 1800 feet

Maps: USDA/FS 7½' Stairs Mtn.;
USGS 7½' Stairs Mtn.

West of the highway (NH 16) through Pinkham Notch and about 8 miles north of Jackson, a high bare ridge supports Glen Boulder among lesser rocks. Outlined against the sky, the great boulder appears about to topple into the notch.

A climb to this landmark also lifts you rapidly to treeline with its strange ecology of ledge and lichen. Glen Boulder is a good destination for an afternoon. Besides being the shortest route to treeline on this eastern side of Mount Washington, it tests your legs and offers a superb panorama of mountainous slopes, valleys, and summits.

How to Get There
The Glen Boulder Trail, cut and marked in 1905, leaves the parking circle and rest rooms at Glen Ellis Falls on the west side of NH 16, 9 miles north of Jackson. (Glen Ellis Falls, reached by a tunnel under the highway and by stone steps into a ravine, sluices spectacularly from a ledge 70 feet into a rocky pool. The water of the Ellis River pours out as from a pitcher. Mist cools the air blowing across the evergreens and the pool, where sightseers click cameras.)

The Trail
The Glen Boulder Trail, rising from the parking area's south corner, slabs across a steep service road and swings right, climbing to level woods. Here you pass through a typical 2000-foot elevation hardwood forest. Big yellow birches, beeches, and other deciduous trees shade striped maples, hobblebushes, and ferns. Wood thrushes and hermit thrushes inhabit the ground and undergrowth.

At the second steep pitch, which takes you to the base of a cliff, the trail

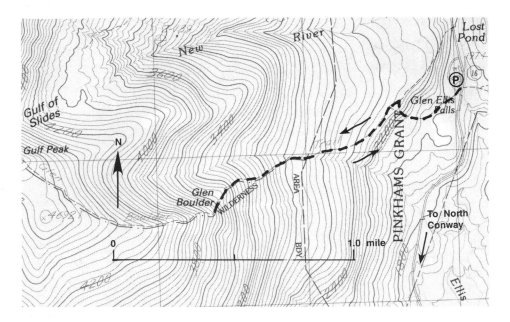

divides. To the left the Chimney Route offers a rugged scramble up a gully and ledges. To the right the Chimney Bypass is the easier route, although steep. I advise choosing it. Just above the cliff the trail takes you to the junction, on your right, with the Direttissima, a trail leading in 1 mile to the Pinkham Notch Visitor Center.

Climbing on, as the Glen Boulder Trail and its orange blazes swing left, you pass after 5 minutes the Chimney Route coming in on your left. Beyond this, a spur trail, left, leads to a view up the notch and across to Wildcat Mountain. The main trail soon begins a steep ascent. Ten minutes above the junction of the Chimney Route, you cross a ski touring trail marked with blue squares. After a half hour of steady climbing, you cross a brook and approach the abruptly rising shoulder. From here you climb from treeline through alpine vegetation, wind-and-snow-flattened black spruce/balsam—known as krummholz—over steep ledges and rocks, for 0.25 mile up to Glen Boulder.

Facing south you look away 20 miles to Mount Chocorua's rocky tower. The sweep is to your left over the Saco River and Ellis River valleys to nearby Wildcat Ridge and around over Pinkham Notch to Mount Washington.

The Glen Boulder Trail continues steeply above treeline and through scrub spruce for more than 1.5 miles to the Davis Path. This fine route to Mount Washington should be undertaken only by seasoned climbers. From Glen Boulder to Mount Washington's summit via the Davis Path and the Crawford Path is a rugged, long 4 miles. A loop to the AMC's Lakes of the Clouds Hut adds another mile. These trails are more difficult than they appear and take longer than you might estimate; allow 3 hours of constant walking and climbing, at least, even in good weather. If there's any sign of clouds descending, rain, or storm, turn around at the boulder and descend to your car.

This is also a warning to the beginner and to the exhilarated devotee who feels a powerful urge to go on just a while longer. You planned a short climb to Glen Boulder. Enjoy yourself there, then head back.

And don't take the Direttissima, or you'll end up at the Pinkham Notch Visitor Center. Keep to the right at that junction.

35

Tuckerman Ravine

Distance (to the Snow Arch and back): 6½ miles

Walking time: 5 hours

Vertical rise: 2300 feet

Maps: USDA/FS 7½' Mt. Washington SE; USGS 7½' x 15' Mt. Washington

A glacial cirque of rocks and cliffs gouged at treeline by prehistoric ice, this dramatic basin in Mount Washington's southeast slope can be an exciting destination as well as the beginning of the strenuous upper climbing to the summit. Open-front shelters amid spruces surround little Hermit Lake. The headwall's precipices are famous for spring skiing when they are banked by tremendous snow accumulations; they drip veils of water that gather at the base to undercut the remaining snow and form the Snow Arch, which survives well into summer.

On the north, the cliff named Lion Head juts into the ravine toward the south wall, which is crowned by Boott Spur. East, from the open half-basin, the view extends across Pinkham Notch to Wildcat Ridge and the Carter Range. Climbing directly from the notch into this giant amphitheater, the Tuckerman Ravine Trail follows a graded tractor path 2.5 miles up to Hermit Lake and the shelters.

How to Get There

Drive north from Jackson on NH 16 for 10 miles until you come to a large sign on the west side identifying the AMC's Pinkham Notch Visitor Center. Turn in and park in the long parking strip, where other hikers, young and old, are preparing to leave for the trails or are returning. Here at the AMC lodge you'll find information on the trails, a snack bar, and other facilities. (Here also you may obtain the permit required if you plan to stay overnight in the ravine's shelters.)

The Trail

To reach the Tuckerman Ravine Trail, walk past the main lodge and turn right. Keep to the wide tractor path. It presents equable grades, but on the upper section leading to the ravine, eroded stones require careful stepping, and it's all uphill. (The descent can be even more taxing on middle-aged knees.)

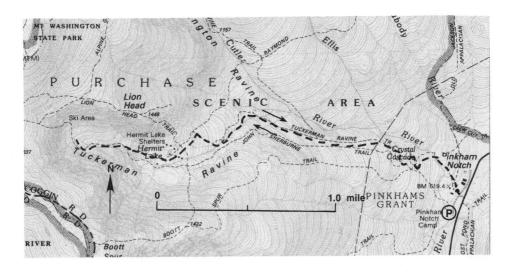

Hikers intending to climb above treeline should take to heart the warning sign about adequate clothing and food and good physical condition.

The path crosses the Cutler River, named soon after the Revolution for an explorer, the Reverend Manasseh Cutler. His party changed the mountain's name from Agiochook to Washington. Beyond the footbridge over this stream whose source is far up under the headwall, you turn a right corner and begin to climb. Soon, on the right again, take a few steps up to a ledge across from Crystal Cascade, one of the most impressive in the mountains.

The path continues to climb by easy switchbacks through a forest of big yellow birch and beech. These woods are favored by the winter wren, in summer only, despite his name. He's notable for his small size and for his vertical tailfeathers. You hear his voluble song more often than you see him in the underbrush.

After about 1 mile, the woods change to spruce and fir interspersed with white birch and mountain ash. You may expect to catch glimpses of boreal chickadees in the evergreens. Their brown caps differentiate them from the common black-capped chickadees. The boreals sing a husky series of notes lacking one or two "dees." Once rare, they seem to have discovered and taken over the cool White Mountains, which lie south of their regular habitat.

Along the Tuckerman Ravine Trail, access links to the John Sherburne Ski Trail occur at intervals on the left. These are marked by signs and can be easily avoided. Stay on the graded tractor path. Continue past the Huntington Ravine Trail, which branches right. Cross a wooden bridge over the Cutler River, where hikers often rest and admire the view toward Wildcat Ridge.

Two miles of steady climbing take you past the Raymond Path on the right and around a wide S-turn into the ravine. You pass the Lion Head Trail, right, and the Boott Spur Link on the left. The ravine opens up to the wide sky and bare rocks. The shelters appear alongside trails and across Hermit Lake.

The central building, known as "Howard Johnson's," burned in 1972,

but has been rebuilt and serves as an information center and caretaker's lodge. No meals are available. The name, applied satirically years ago to an earlier building that also burned, expressed the attitude of various salty characters who preferred the primitive ravine when it had only two log shelters. Cliffs tower above, and, to the west, beyond a rocky slope edged with scrub spruce, the headwall rises perpendicularly toward the clouds that coast steadily eastward.

The open-front shelters are for the 86 overnight hikers who obtain permits at the Pinkham Notch Visitor Center. There is a small fee. Overuse of the limited area, as throughout the mountains at certain popular spots, has made new regulations necessary. Camping in the woods has been discontinued to preserve the delicate subalpine soil, trees, and plant life. Hikers should bring their own lunches and carry out their own trash. If cooking is planned, they should carry portable stoves; wood or charcoal fires are not allowed. The endangered ecology is responding to these conservation measures; hikers realize the problem and help.

A 0.75-mile climb over a trail now rough and rocky leads you to the headwall and the Snow Arch. (This is still Tuckerman Ravine Trail continuing from the shelter areas on the north or right side of the brook.) Never walk under the Snow Arch. Huge chunks fall off without warning. By late summer it has melted away into the Cutler River.

The Tuckerman Ravine Trail finds a route over rocks at the base of the cliffs, and circles the headwall to the north of the cliffs. Hikers on holiday weekends form a moving line of figures on the trail up and across the headwall. Balmy weather in the ravine sometimes changes to icy wind and clouds above; plan on its doing so.

The summit of Mount Washington is only 1 mile from the Snow Arch, but it's a mile to remember. Time is a better measure: 2 hours, if you are accustomed to scrambling over rocks at such an angle. The 1000 feet up to the summit from the diverging trails above the headwall (known as Tuckerman Junction) appear less because above treeline there is no familiar sight for estimating distance. The landscape is as strange as the sudden storms are fierce. And the higher you climb the fiercer they get; the protection of the ravine is often welcome.

Tuckerman Ravine

36

Mount Washington

Distance (round trip): 9 miles

Walking time: 9 hours

Vertical rise: 3675 feet

Maps: USDA/FS 7½' Mt. Washington SE; USGS 7½' x 15' Mt. Washington

By its western approach, the route of this climb to Mount Washington takes you up the steep and scenic Ammonoosuc Ravine from near the cog railway's base station. Just above treeline, the AMC's Lakes of the Clouds Hut offers shelter if the weather turns frigid and stormy. Mount Washington's rocky cone and the summit buildings tower 1200 feet higher and 1.5 miles away at the top of the trail laid out by the legendary mountaineer, Ethan Allen Crawford.

On the summit, you'll meet tourists who came on the cog railway or in their cars. They think you are out of your mind for climbing when you could ride. For the dyed-in-the-wool hiker, once or twice on the summit is enough, unforgettable as it is.

Save this climb for a day of match-less clarity, so rare on this peak of cloud, rain, and storm. Waiting for a clear day will prove worthwhile. Then the far horizon will be the limit of vision, and you'll see a great sweep of country that includes most of New Hampshire and parts of Maine, Vermont, and the Province of Quebec. You will stand at the center of a circle 200 miles in diameter, enclosing hundreds of mountains and valleys in 30,000 square miles. Perhaps you'll see the ocean to the east, blending with the sky.

How to Get There
Leave US 302 at Fabyan and drive on the Base Road 7.25 miles to hiker parking on the right. You are 0.25 mile west of the base station.

The Trail
The Ammonoosuc Ravine Trail starts at the east side of the large parking area. A bulletin board displays trail information provided by the forest service and the AMC. Shoulder your pack. It should contain a heavy sweater, a thick wool shirt or insulated jacket, and a parka, warm cap, and gloves. Rain gear is good insurance. Your lunch and water should

Ball Crag

MT. WASHINGTON STATE PARK

ANDROSCOGGIN R

SACO

TUC...

Ski A...

BM 1371.4

1861

BM 1916.6

Radio Towers

(WHOM-WMTW)

GREAT GULF

Mt Spaulding Clay Lake

Water Tanks

WESTSIDE TRAIL

Mt Washington TRAIL

PATH

CROSSOVER

1637

CAMEL TRAIL

Lakes of the Clouds

N

Mt Clay MT CLAY LOOP TR

APPALACHIAN GULFSIDE

Gulfside Tr

I

S

A

R

G

E

N

T

S

P

U

R

D

TUCKERMAN

CRAWFORD

1660

1410

Lakes of the Clouds Hut

AMMONOOSUC

DR

1.0 mile

TRAIL

Burt Ravine

RAILROAD

Water Tank

COG

578

Monroe Brook

TRAIL

AMMONOOSUC

Brook

JEWELL

882

0

N

Brook

Marshfield Sta

River

Franklin

Brook

ROAD

302

770.8

Base Station

CHANDLERS

PURCHASE

BM 783.0

BOUNDARY LINE

TRAIL

CLAY

JEFFERSON NOTCH

Brook

Ammonoosuc

ROAD

BASE GRADE

Sokokis

ANS

be supplemented by emergency food for two meals. If you climb in shorts, carry warm pants. You are heading for an arctic-alpine zone.

This new parking in the woods restricts the views that were so impressive approaching the former trailhead at the base station. From there, the barren heights rise to desolate rocks and make you acutely aware of the rugged ascent. At the new start in the woods you are less likely to evaluate your fitness realistically. Also missing, besides the challenging view, is the busy scene around the station where gala-clad vacationers watch engineers in overalls, grimy firemen and brakemen, or visit the gift shop and snack bar while awaiting train time. Engines with tilted boilers puff smoke and steam from coal fires and push passenger cars up the steep track by means of a drive gear engaging the steel pins set between the two walls of a center rail. This was the invention of New Hampshire–born Sylvester March. In 1869 President Ulysses S. Grant rode up the mountain on the first train, along with P.T. Barnum, who allowed that the next morning's sunrise was the "second greatest show on earth." (No overnight accommodations now.)

The Ammonoosuc Ravine Trail leads up an easy slope from the parking area into a forest of spruce, fir, and birch. After 0.25 mile, Franklin Brook is a stone-to-stone crossing. Beyond this gully are two old water pipes leading to the base station. Then the trail swings southeast away from the sound of steam engines and descends to its former route, about 0.75 mile from your car. Keep to the right up this old path beside the Ammonoosuc River. In the next mile you pass a tributary brook and continue to Gem Pool below a fine waterfall.

Across the stream you begin the precipitous ascent up steps among spruces. The trail faces you like a rough, rocky wall of earth reinforced with tree roots. Partway up this first steep section, a small sign and a spur trail on the right offer you the opportunity to see the brook's glittering torrent pour down a long stone sluice formed by ledges. Climbing on up the main trail, you pass wide carpets of green-leaved wood sorrel, which blooms white in mid-July. You come to another high falls where at this altitude the mountain or alpine avens blooms yellow in early July. Among open rocks, Labrador tea puts out white frilly flowers, and bog laurel shows pink blooms above moist turf.

Ten minutes climbing brings you to another falls and brook crossing, then soon to another. The spruces dwindle to the ancient dwarf clumps twisted and flattened by winds at treeline. The scrub growth ends at the vast expanse of rocks, which extends to Mount Washington's summit on your left. Follow cairns and blue paint blazes the last 100 yards over the ledges to the Lakes of the Clouds Hut on the windswept col between Mount Washington and Mount Monroe on your right.

This AMC hut is the largest (excluding the headquarters at the Pinkham Notch Visitor Center) in the hut system. Stone walls first withstood the gales at 5050 feet in 1915. Now expanded and modernized with a capacity of 90 guests, the hut is a popular stopover. Many hikers cross from the Tuckerman Ravine Trail, descend from Mount Washington, or traverse the 7-mile ridge from Crawford Notch. The hut is the terminus of the Ammonoosuc Ravine Trail.

Here the wind, and often clouds in the form of dense fog, as well as vio-

Lakes of the Clouds Hut

lent summer storms of rain, lightning, and sleet, decide for you whether or not you climb on toward the summit on this try. You will probably understand why unwary hikers above treeline on Mount Washington have perished from exposure in the summer.

When the weather's favorable, take the Crawford Path from the hut and follow it between two little lakes whose stony shores and ledges support alpine plants, sedges, and shrubs. These botanical miracles possess the unbelievable tenacity of mountain flora as long as nature's delicate balance remains undisturbed. Varieties of heaths such as alpine bilberry and mountain cranberry survive doggedly in niches of scant earth.

Beyond the second lake, on rising ground, the Camel Trail branches right to Boott Spur, and the Tuckerman Crossover leads to Tuckerman Junction above the ravine. Keep on the Crawford Path. It is well worn. It is marked by cairns, each topped with a yellow-painted rock. The gradual climb here is straight toward Washington's summit. The Davis Path joins from the right as you near the actual ascent of the cone. Not far beyond, the Westside Trail splits left to circle the cone for climbers heading toward the northern peaks of the Presidential Range—Clay, Jefferson, Adams, and Madison. Watch for this fork and be sure to bear right; although the cairn markers are the same, there's no chance of confusion in clear weather.

Mount Washington's summit beckons 0.5 mile ahead. You pass patches of tough Bigelow sedge, which thrives in this exposed situation. Juncos also appear at home. Now you go up the cone in a passage among rocks. You climb the final shoulder and look away to the northern peaks. The Gulfside Trail comes in left from these peaks. You approach the summit from the north up the last rock slope.

Your introduction to the modern age on the summit can be jarring—television towers, transmitter buildings, two monster cylinders rising like rocket launchers, a railroad with steam engine and passenger car, the occupants from the train and tourists from the auto road wandering around, the old stone-walled Tip Top House still preserved for its history—all appear insignificant compared to the extensive Sherman Adams Building partially encircling the actual summit. You are in the 59-acre Mount Washington State Park. The top of the world in northeastern America is a ledge behind the Sherman Adams Building, 6288 feet above sea level.

Inside the commodious building you'll find shelter from the wind, and wide views through the windows that curve around the lobby–dining room. You can visit the cafeteria, gift shop, museum, and information desk. The Mount Washington Observatory, a weather station, is also housed under the roof of concrete slabs.

If you are lucky enough to reach the summit early on a perfectly clear day and are fit for the challenge of more above-treeline balancing on rocks, you may want to descend by the Gulfside Trail and the Jewell Trail, as a loop back to your car. (Or you may *climb* by the Jewell Trail. It starts from the Base Road opposite the hiker parking.)

The Gulfside Trail, which in sections could almost be described as paved with stones, takes you past the headwall of the awesome Great Gulf, the largest glacial cirque on Mount Washington. The Jewell Trail joins the Gulfside at the west slope of Mount

Clay. Unlike the Gulfside, the Jewell Trail's upper section is composed of rugged slabs marked in yellow paint. Above the evergreen scrub, the trail is marked by cairns. Below treeline, the trail is a graded way, but don't attempt it in bad weather. While the views are magnificent, caution should guide your mountaineering on dangerous old Mount Washington.

Unless you choose the Gulfside-Jewell variation, descend as you came up by the Crawford Path and Ammonoosuc Ravine Trail.

37

The Alpine Garden

Distance (round trip): 8½ miles

Walking time: 6½ hours

Vertical rise: 3500 feet

Maps: USDA/FS 7½' Mt. Washington SE; USGS 7½' x 15' Mt. Washington

The object of the climb to Mount Washington's Alpine Garden is enjoyment of the mountain rather than its conquest. This loop climb, with the garden as its destination, is a rugged and demanding rock-scramble above treeline. But it's spectacular and shows you why the mountain is unique. The alpine-arctic environment at the garden affords more attractions than the tourist mecca on the summit.

Despite its barren appearance, this mile-high garden displays many of the 110 plant species that live above treeline on Mount Washington and other Presidential peaks. Of this total, 75 are never found below these altitudes in New Hampshire. Most of the alpine plants occur at lower elevations in Alaska, northern Canada, Greenland, and arctic Eurasia.

The flower time, mid-June to July, brings the Alpine Garden a miraculous shower of colors. Then you see yellow alpine avens, white diapensia, purple Lapland rosebay, and pink bilberry. The grasses, such as Bigelow sedge and three-forked rush, sprout new green blades.

The Alpine Garden's plateau interrupts Mount Washington's steep eastern slope. A curving, mile-long shelf between Tuckerman Ravine and Huntington Ravine, the garden begins and ends above these tremendous gorges. You look into dizzying depths and contrast them with the spaciousness of the sweeping views across Pinkham Notch to the Carter and Wildcat Ranges.

How to Get There
The climb to this elemental world begins at the AMC's Pinkham Notch Visitor Center 10 miles north of Jackson on NH 16. Park in the parking area.

The Trail
Walk past the lodge and turn right onto the Tuckerman Ravine Trail. Follow this path for about 300 feet and watch on your right for the trail

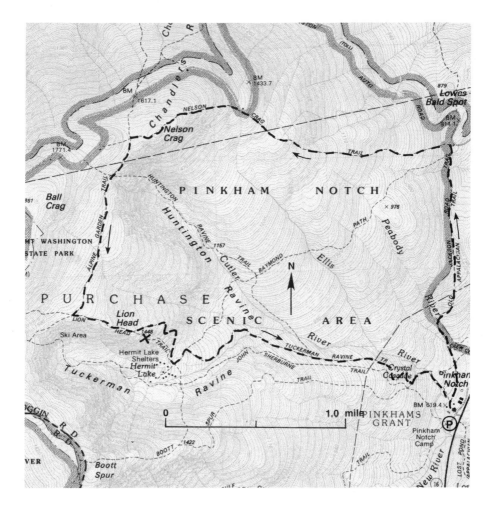

to the Old Jackson Road. This ancient wagon road, now a trail and part of the AT marked as usual with the white blazes, takes you straight through a junction with the Blanchard and Connie's Way ski trails and past the Crew Cut Trail and then George's Gorge Trail, while crossing several brooks, before ascending to a sharp left turn off the old grade onto a trail cut in 1977. (This avoids any climbing on the auto road, which was formerly required.)

On rock steps the trail rises steeply for a short distance. Then you pass the Raymond Path on your left—it leads to the Tuckerman Ravine Trail. Next, at 1.7 mile, you come to the Nelson Crag Trail. Turn left onto it. (For more information about the trail ahead and beyond the auto road see Hike 33, Lowe's Bald Spot.)

The Nelson Crag Trail heads west and almost at once goes directly at the mountain. This steep section leads you for a mile through evergreens, which become scrub at an open ridge with views of Pinkham Notch. Turning north over rocks, it joins the auto road above the 5-mile marker, and returns, left, to the rugged rocks on the side of Nelson Crag, which is not a single rock but a pile of huge rock slabs. A large cairn tells you that you've mastered the climb. Beyond the cairn you come to the Alpine Garden Trail between the auto road and Tuckerman Ravine. You are nearly a mile above sea level. (The Nelson Crag Trail continues beyond, bearing left across the Huntington Ravine Trail, over a rocky crest to crossings of the auto road and the cog railway before reaching the summit.)

At the junction with the Alpine Garden Trail take a good look at the weather. If you have any inkling that it will deteriorate in the next few hours or even if you are encountering ordinary clouds that are common above treeline, there is no point in continuing. The Alpine Garden is a gloomy rock field in cloud, and the cloud may be a warning of the deadly storms that blast Mount Washington. To retreat, turn right (north) on the Alpine Garden Trail and follow it to the auto road. Follow the auto road down to the Old Jackson Road for the return to Pinkham Notch Visitor Center.

But, of course, if you've picked a clear day for this climb, the skies are blue and the sun is dazzling. In that happy event, turn left (south) from the Nelson Crag Trail onto the Alpine Garden Trail.

Soon you descend over rocks with views of Huntington Ravine on your left and the cone of Mount Washington on your right. A great cairn marks the junction with the Huntington Ravine Trail. Keep straight across. (The Huntington Ravine Trail climbs right 0.25 mile to the auto road. To your left, it descends over the dangerous rocks in the ravine.) Now you are in the Alpine Garden, and ahead stretches the mile of scattered, broken stones among which grow the dwarf spruces, alpine plants, and shrubs. A pause for lunch gives you time to look about and absorb both the desolation and the life on this plateau, where plants not only survive but blossom in colors to match the rainbow.

(Warning note: Don't pluck or disturb the plants; they're unique, and they're protected. Don't drink from the little brook that crosses the Alpine Garden; it's contaminated by drainage from the summit.)

As you proceed, keep to the Alpine Garden Trail. Follow the cairns. The trail's worn rocks and tracked soil will guide you if a cloud descends—but pay attention. You cross a broad flat as you approach Tuckerman Ravine and the intersection with the Lion Head Trail. (The Alpine Garden Trail continues another 0.25 mile to the Tuckerman Ravine Trail.)

Turn left on the Lion Head Trail for magnificent views along the rim of Tuckerman Ravine. In June you will probaby gaze down at skiers on late snow in the ravine. The trail leads you over Lion Head's granite brow to a descent of its bare eastern shoulder. You step down from reinforcing logs at frequent intervals as the trail curves to your right into evergreen scrub and the lower spruce/fir woods. At the junction with the Tuckerman Ravine Trail, turn left. The trail is a tractor road here, leading you 2.25 miles down to the Pinkham Notch Visitor Center, but the upper part is eroded to a bed of stones. If your legs are tired don't try to hurry.

38

Mount Jefferson

Distance (round trip): 5 miles

Walking time: 5½ hours

Vertical rise: 2700 feet

Maps: USDA/FS 7½' Mt. Washington SE; USGS 7½' x 15' Mt. Washington

The sensational view south from Mount Jefferson's summit owes its fame to a vast glacial cirque, the Great Gulf, backed by the towering crags of Mount Washington. A remote peak of the Presidential Range if approached from the north, south, or east, and the third highest at 5712 feet, Jefferson conceals its western access under the spruces that grow in Jefferson Notch. There the Caps Ridge Trail leaves the road and surmounts a sharp, west spur for the 2.5-mile climb to the summit. Caps Ridge, however, should be approached warily rather than with the assurance that you've found the mountain's weak spot. The Caps Ridge Trail ascends the equivalent of a vertical 0.5 mile.

The ledges, or Caps, challenge your legs and lungs. And the Caps present treacherous footing during or after a rainstorm.

How to Get There
To reach Jefferson Notch, turn off US 302 at Fabyan and follow the road toward the cog railway's base station. Drive about 5 miles to an intersection. Turn left there onto the Jefferson Notch Road (gravel). Careful driving and occasional use of low gear take you 3 miles up to 3008 feet. You are at the height-of-land on the road, where the Caps Ridge trailhead is the highest trailhead on a public road in the White Mountains. Park in the parking areas on the right or left.

The Trail
The Caps Ridge Trail leads east through green spruce/fir woods. Leaving behind this wet and rooty section, you begin the real climb. Soon you catch glimpses of Mount Clay on the right.

About 1 mile into the hike the view opens at a smooth ledge, right, in which small potholes indicate glacial action. Continue up 100 yards and pass the Link Trail on the left.

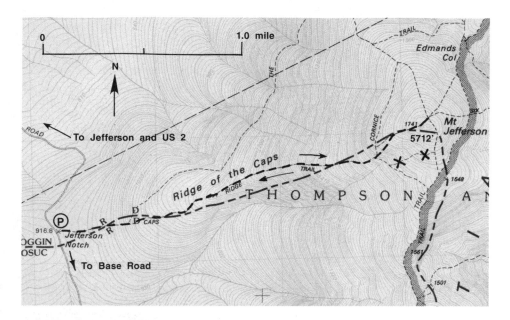

The evergreens become smaller as the trail rises steeply among jumbled rocks. You clamber up to treeline below the first of two jagged ledges called the Caps. About 0.25 mile above, as the ridge becomes a sawtooth edge, you climb the second Cap. You are exposed to all the mountains and the sky. You're also exposed to the weather. If you see signs of rain, fog, or high winds, turn back while you can.

Climbing on under clear skies, you descend from the last Cap and start up the broad main peak. You cross the Cornice Trail, which for a few yards joins your Caps Ridge Trail. (The Cornice Trail, avoiding Jefferson's summit, offers a rough route left, north, to Edmands Col. To the right it swings southeast and joins the Gulfside Trail.) Here on the mountainside, open to the most violent and frigid winds, grasslike sedges and rushes thrive in little slanting meadows among acres of broken rock. In the fall—August at this altitude—these green swaths change to soft, pale tan colors.

Above the Cornice intersection, you may guess the next rise to be the summit, but you climb over two more before the cairns lead slightly left up the summit crags. Now you discover that Jefferson's summit consists of three crests bordering a lower flat, where signs mark the trail junction.

Each crest gives you an interesting perspective across the Great Gulf toward Mount Washington, its auto road, and summit buildings. The southeast ledges overlook the Gulfside Trail's yellow-topped cairns crossing above the two ridges known as Jefferson's Knees. Looking east across Edmands Col to Mount Adams, you notice that it hides the last peak in the range, Mount Madison. (Note: The emergency shelter at Edmands Col east of Mount Jefferson on the Gulfside Trail has been removed.)

After lunch on the summit, return over the Caps down to Jefferson Notch and your car.

39

Mount Adams

Distance (round trip): 9 miles

Walking time: 7½ hours

Vertical rise: 4500 feet

Maps: USDA/FS 7½' Mt. Washington SE; USGS 7½' x 15' Mt. Washington

Mount Adams fascinates and challenges many hikers more than any peak in the Presidential Range. It offers deep ravines and long ridges. Majestic views across the Great Gulf toward Mount Washington greet you from the summit crags. Mounts Jefferson and Madison seem like neighbors. Second in height to Washington at 5774 feet, Mount Adams when climbed from the north demands 231 more vertical feet than Mount Washington from Pinkham Notch. This ruggedness guarantees no tourists.

The shortest trail up Mount Adams begins at Appalachia, a former railroad flagstop that is now a parking space south of US 2. The Air Line Trail goes straight up prominent Durand Ridge.

How to Get There

Take US 2 west from Gorham's traffic lights. Drive 5.5 miles over Gorham Hill and across the Moose River. You identify Appalachia on the left (south) by the row of hikers' cars even before you see the sign TRAILS PARKING.

The Trail

Facing the mountains, take the path from the right-hand corner of the parking area. Cross the Boston and Maine tracks. The path forks, Valley Way bearing left, Air Line right. Keep to the right under the powerline. At the edge of the woods is a sign for Air Line. You enter maple woods. Various trails, for which you have seen signs, begin to branch from both sides of Air Line. You pass the Link and Amphibrach. Next, you pass the crossing of Sylvan Way, then later, Beechwood Way. Then Short Line branches right, and you cross Randolph Path, all in the first mile. Keep on Air Line.

The trail goes up soon enough. Expect an abrupt rise beyond a spring on your left off the trail. The steep and uneven section of the trail takes you up Durand Ridge. You pass the junction of the Scar Trail coming in on the

Mount Adams, from Mount Jefferson

left, then after 0.5 mile you pass Upper Bruin; both trails connect to Valley Way in the valley of Snyder Brook.

Durand Ridge, reaching above treeline, sharpens to the Knife Edge. You clamber past rocks that overlook the precipitous King Ravine on your right.

From the ravine comes a trail, Chemin des Dames ("Ladies' Road"), which is the "easy" way up from that mysterious giant gorge named for its 1857 explorer, the Reverend Starr King. You look down upon rocks the size of houses. Hidden in caves under them, ice never melts. The ravine, by legend, is the resting place for a starving band of Rogers's Rangers retreating after their retaliatory attack on the St. Francis Indian Village in Canada during the French and Indian War.

Air Line next takes you past a branch trail, left, to the AMC's Madison Hut, which is situated near the barren col between Mount Adams and Mount Madison. You keep on Air Line and climb steeply past the King Ravine Trail, right, at an entrance between ledges forming the Gateway into that glacial cirque.

Air Line joins the Gulfside Trail, coming in at the left, and they merge for a few yards. Mount Madison is in full view northeast.

(If you're caught by one of the notable Mount Adams thunderstorms, which feature virtuoso lightning bolts, and your hair seems inclined to stand on end, turn left onto the Gulfside Trail for a descent to shelter at Madison Hut. Yellow-painted stones top Gulfside cairns.)

The Air Line Trail soon forks left off the Gulfside Trail. (Gulfside continues around Mount Adams toward Mount Jefferson and Mount Washing-

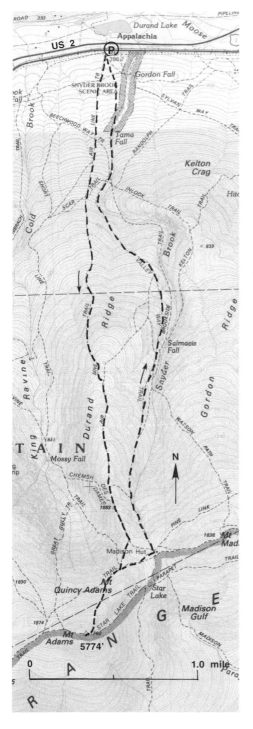

ton.) Air Line climbs past a minor summit, on the left, named John Quincy Adams for the sixth president, and takes you up among rock slabs to the main peak of Mount Adams.

The summit spreads out before you a tremendous view into the Great Gulf. You feel as though you are leaning over the abyss, not because of sheer cliffs but because of the vastness. Mount Washington's superior height and size dominate the south outlook; the summit buildings are 3.5 miles away. Across the Gulf on a winding ribbon up the slopes, small bugs, which are cars, creep along the auto road. At the horizon to your right, Mount Jefferson stands jagged against the sky; to your left, Mount Madison. Turning around northward, you see below you a lesser crest, named for the revolutionary of the Adams family—Sam Adams—and rising beyond is Thunderstorm Junction, where the Gulfside Trail meets other trails at a huge cairn. In this north view on a clear day, you see the two bare Percy Peaks in the distance and the ridges near the Canadian border. More to the east, Umbagog Lake sparkles in the forest at the end of Maine's Rangeley Lakes chain.

For your descent, retrace your steps down Air Line as far as the Gulfside Trail. Keep past the place where Air Line forks left and stay on Gulfside for the steep drop into evergreen scrub near Madison Hut. The Gulfside Trail ends at the hut.

Take the Valley Way Trail for your return to Appalachia. Valley Way descends rapidly into the Snyder Brook valley and offers protection from storms after you enter the woods. Follow it past and across several trails, until it joins Air Line as you complete the loop and approach Appalachia.

40

Mount Madison

Distance (round trip): 10½ miles

Walking time: 8 hours

Vertical rise: 3800 feet

Maps: USDA/FS 7½' Mt. Washington SE; USGS 7½' x 15' Mt. Washington; USDA/FS 7½' Carter Dome; USGS 7½' Carter Dome

This rock pyramid completes the Presidential Range's northern peaks. Tourists and hikers alike see its bare crags towering above the northern approach to Pinkham Notch. Of its 5367 feet, 4500 rise directly from the Androscoggin River valley. It juts above treeline into the alpine-arctic environment of fragmented rock slabs, cold fogs, wind, and scanty vegetation. The peak is particularly impressive from NH 16 near the entrance to the Mount Washington Auto Road, where the Osgood Trail formerly began. Hikers for a hundred years enjoyed this scenic trail to Mount Madison's summit. They continue to do so, but from a 1985 parking area and an approach via the Great Gulf Trail.

Fine views on Osgood Ridge from treeline upward extend south and west into the Great Gulf, across to Mount Washington, and along the range that sweeps over Mount Jefferson and Mount Adams to Madison. The route of this hike includes not only Osgood Ridge and Mount Madison's summit, but also the AMC's Madison Hut and a return loop through Madison Gulf. The climb should be saved for a shining clear day.

How to Get There
Drive 1.6 miles north of the entrance to the Mount Washington Auto Road. At a large sign for the Great Gulf Wilderness turn west off NH 16. The parking area along the bank of the Peabody River was once the route of NH 16. With your pack equipped for a climb into the alpine-arctic zone, walk across the footbridge spanning the river.

The Trail
The trail beyond the bridge leads up a slight grade among hemlocks to the Great Gulf Trail from the Dolly Copp Campground, 2 miles north of your car via NH 16. Turn left onto the Great Gulf Trail. Soon you will be walking

above the rushing torrents and pools of the Peabody River's West Branch. At times the Great Gulf Trail coincides with sections of the Hayes Copp Ski Touring Trail from the campground.

The ski trail is blazed with small squares of blue plastic, not to be confused with blue paint blazes of the Great Gulf Trail. Three bridges and skier logo signs accommodate your brook crossings and direct you. Stay on the Great Gulf Trail.

After a mile of this pleasant woods walk your path bears away from the stream. You come to a junction of the ski trail branching north. In 15 minutes more you arrive at the Osgood Trail on your right, also northward. This trail will be your route to Mount Madison. (The Great Gulf Trail continues straight ahead.)

Turn right onto the Osgood Trail. You walk up an easy slope among beech and yellow birch, spruce and balsam. If you listen you can hear, down in the valley, the West Branch pouring over boulders and into pools.

Before the Osgood Trail takes you to serious climbing, it crosses a small brook and then brings you to an important junction. On your left the

Osgood Cutoff enters. Take notice because you'll return here as you complete your loop from the Madison Gulf Trail via this Osgood Cutoff. (On your right, almost under a big boulder, a spur trail passes a spring and ends at tent platforms.)

Continue ahead on the Osgood Trail. You can start climbing in earnest. This steep section must be dealt with by the patience formula: one boot in front of the other. You climb through fine spruce woods. You're on a section of the Appalachian Trail, and you are also following the boundary of the White Mountain National Forest's 5552-acre Great Gulf Wilderness.

The spruces diminish in size; they become sparse and scattered. You look up from your climbing and find yourself in the wind and skies among rocks that rise ahead crest after crest.

Pause here and try to predict the weather. Fierce gales blast Osgood Ridge, and storms come up rapidly. It's a long, rugged, unsheltered mile over a series of high rock piles. You can easily turn back here.

Fair skies and breezes are the signal to continue to climb up the craggy peaks. Follow the cairns among the

Madison Hut

ROBERT J. KOZLOW

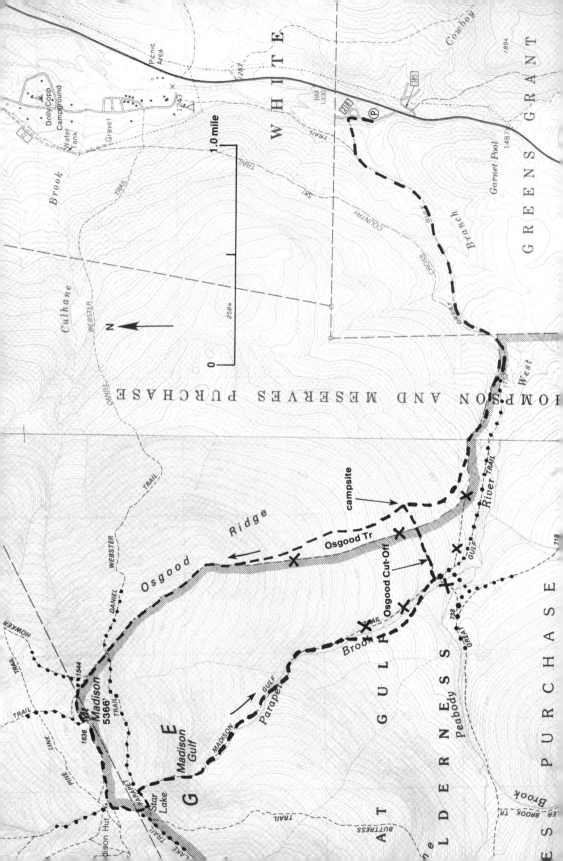

rock slabs and over the ledges. You are on the crest of Osgood Ridge, which curves left as well as up. You climb down a few yards over massive rocks to a narrow east-west flat. Trail signs mark this as Osgood Junction. The Daniel Webster Trail comes in on the right from the Dolly Copp Campground. On the left, the Parapet Trail offers a 1-mile circuit below Madison's summit to Madison Hut. (Very acceptable in a sudden rainstorm.)

The Osgood Trail goes up steeply again over the rocks along the ridge to Madison's northeast shoulder. It swings left down into a brief level section before the climb up the final pinnacle. On rising rocks again, you pass the Howker Ridge Trail, right. The Osgood Trail winds up westward among broken ledges.

At the summit, you stand on the big rocks that mark the end of the Presidential Range. The mountainside plunges northward into the valley. In that direction, the Watson Path drops off the summit. To the southeast you look down at the auto road entrance. Clouds may come pouring out of the northwest before you have studied Mount Washington and the cars rounding the auto road's corner called the Horn, which you see across the Great Gulf. Mount Adams on the west often catches cloud wisps or disappears entirely.

The return route begins on the summit as part of a loop into Madison Gulf. Keep west on the Osgood Trail along the jagged ridge beyond Madison's summit. The trail, marked by cairns, bears left off the ridge and descends the shoulder to Madison Hut below the looming crags of Mount Adams. The stone hut, where AMC "croo" members provide meals and lodging for 50 hikers, serves also as a terminus for the Osgood Trail and various trails north and west.

Your route leaves the hut, south, by the Parapet Trail. Climb up the slope and keep left at the branch trail to tiny Star Lake. Across the col, the Parapet Trail makes a sharp left turn as you approach the lookoff ledges. Then it descends into a gully and the Madison Gulf Trail begins, right. (The Parapet Trail keeps on toward Osgood Junction.) Turn right onto the Madison Gulf Trail. Climb down carefully over the steep, slippery rocks among scrub spruces. *Warning:* The footing can be treacherous. Be prepared to take a lot of time.

The trail descends the Gulf by abrupt pitches between more gradual traverses, with many crossings of Parapet Brook. About 1.5 hours from treeline, you make the last crossing over the brook's smooth rocks, to the east bank, and climb to a trail junction. Your route, the Osgood Cutoff, leads ahead toward the Osgood Trail. (The Madison Gulf Trail bears right down to the Great Gulf Trail.)

The Osgood Cutoff stays on a slabbing curve along the 2500-foot contour through open woods. In about 15 minutes you'll see the sign for the Osgood Trail junction. Turn right down the now familiar route to the Great Gulf Trail, where you turn left and continue to retrace the morning's path. Avoid the ski touring trail sections. Watch for the branch trail to the right leading to the suspension bridge. (The Great Gulf Trail keeps on to the Dolly Copp Campground.)

Soon you can again admire the engineering of the bridge. Beyond it you'll welcome your car and its four wheels to carry you.

41

Mount Kearsarge North

Distance (round trip): 6 miles

Walking time: 5 hours

Vertical rise: 2600 feet

Maps: USDA/FS 7½' North Conway East; USGS 15' North Conway

If you start climbing Mount Kearsarge North at dawn and if the day stays clear, you'll see the shining wet rocks of Tuckerman Ravine's headwall 16 miles north on Mount Washington; to the right, Lion Head's cliff glows, and Huntington Ravine's rock facade catches sunlight in a bright chasm.

Maps show the mountain as Kearsarge North, which distinguishes it from the Kearsarge near Warner. The former name, Mount Pequawket, is all but forgotten. The Pequawket Native Americans hunted and raised corn in the Conway-Fryeburg forests and meadows along the Saco River.

Mount Kearsarge North became a popular summit for white men after 1845, when three enterprising men cut a bridle path to the 3268-foot top and built a two-story wooden inn. The structure survived many years until an autumn gale blew it loose from its iron mooring rods and chains. Rebuilt, it stood for 25 more years before the winds blew it apart. A 1951-vintage fire tower now occupies the summit ledge, but, like others in the mountains, it is no longer manned by a lone watcher; air patrols have taken over.

If you climb Mount Kearsarge North in the fall after snow has dusted the Presidentials, you'll understand the note on an 18th-century map issued during the French and Indian War, when this land was known only to hunters, trappers, and Native Americans. The note read "These WHITE HILLS appear many Leagues off at Sea like great bright Clouds above the Horizon, & are a noted Land Mark to Seamen."

How to Get There
Drive about 2 miles north from North Conway on NH 16. Pass the scenic outlook to Mount Washington. Cross the railroad tracks and turn right onto the Hurricane Mountain Road. Drive through Kearsarge Village. Less than

0.5 mile beyond, the Mount Kearsarge North Trail starts on the left at a trail sign and small parking area.

The Trail
The trail enters the woods and traverses tree-grown fields of the former Eastman farm; once a shady lane led to the house and barn. Steven Eastman built this lower trail through his pasture about 1872 as a link to the bridle path at Prospect Ledge. Now the farm has returned to forest.

The true ascent begins after the first 0.5 mile. Steadily upward the trail progresses through hardwoods of maple, beech, and birch to open rocks sparsely grown to sumacs and evergreens. You follow cairns and paint marks over slanting Prospect Ledge. There are wide views to the Saco valley south and west.

In the woods again, climb on for another half hour along an ascending forest trail to more open ledges and scattered trees. Gradually you pass the minor wooded summit, Bartlett Mountain, on your left and swing north and cast around ledges again. Turning south for the final climb, you follow cairns and worn paths up the last rocks among spruces to the summit ledge and tower. You first look straight ahead to Maine and its lakes. Then you turn left, and the Presidential Range takes all your attention.

To descend from the summit, follow the trail you climbed. A leisurely pace will show you many plants and trees that you could have missed in eagerness to reach the summit. First, the vines of mountain cranberry climb to crevices only a few yards from the tower. Soon, to the right, crowberry, another subalpine plant, creeps over hummocks in the scrub evergreens. During late June and early July, sheep laurel blooms pink and showy. Crum-

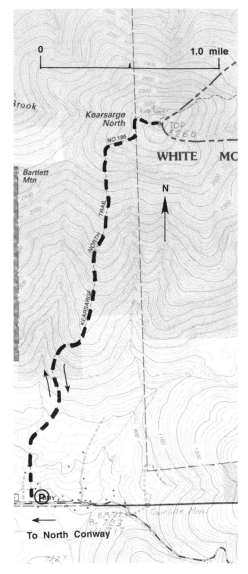

bled rock fragments support three-toothed cinquefoil. The trail offers examples of the predominant conifers in the White Mountains—magnificent white pines, red pines, balsam fir, red spruce, and the long aisles of a hemlock forest above the brook.

For full appreciation, Mount Kearsarge North requires several visits.

42

Tom-Field-Avalon Loop

Distance (round trip): 8 miles
Walking time: 6 hours
Vertical rise: 2800 feet
Maps: USDA/FS 7½' Crawford Notch; USGS 7½' Crawford Notch

Trails south from Crawford Notch link Mount Tom, Mount Field, and Mount Avalon for a loop hike. Spruces cloak Mount Field and Mount Tom, but both summits reach above 4000 feet: Mount Tom, 4047 feet, and Mount Field, 4326 feet. Mount Avalon, a bare rock escarpment at 3450 feet, overlooks Crawford Notch toward Webster Cliff and Mount Washington.

How to Get There
Drive to the site of the Crawford House on US 302 at the northern end of the notch. East of this, and south of Saco Lake's west end, the old railroad depot is an information center maintained by the AMC, which acquired the land and remaining buildings around the Crawford House after it was dismantled and burned in 1977. Park near the depot.

The Trail
The Avalon Trail, your first section of the loop, begins across the Conway Scenic Railroad tracks south of the depot. Step over the tracks and cross a narrow, neglected field to the entrance into the woods.

Your loop hike will take you up the Avalon Trail to the A-Z Trail and Mount Tom Spur, then the Willey Range Trail to Mount Field, back down the Avalon Trail to Mount Avalon, and the return to your car at Crawford Depot.

A wide path through the woods, the Avalon Trail soon leads you past the trail on the left to Mount Willard, which offers less ambitious members of a party a spectacular view for 1.5 miles of upgrade. Shortly you come to the valley's brook and cross. Up the west bank you begin the real climb. You pass on your left the lower and upper junctions of a bypass trail for viewing cascades. A ledge farther on, and left, gives a breathing place above The Pool.

About half an hour from your car, the trail leads to the right, west of the

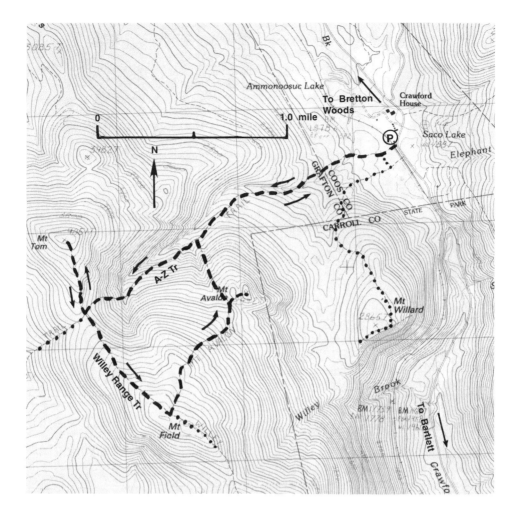

old path higher on the bank, and takes you to the second crossing of the brook. You are climbing toward the steep end of the valley, which is essentially a glacial cirque with a wooded headwall. Many waterbars and steps have been built into the trail. Watch for the A-Z Trail. It forks right on an ascent where the upper rim of the cirque appears in that direction. Take the A-Z Trail. (You will return to this junction as you near the end of your hike.)

The A-Z Trail drops into and climbs out of a rough gully, then angles up for 0.5 mile to the last trickling brook. You begin the steep, rough 0.5-mile climb that takes you up to the height-of-land between Mount Tom and Mount Field.

A spur trail leads right for the 0.75-mile climb to Mount Tom's summit. It winds through a tunnel in the evergreens into young leafy trees alternating with spruce and fir. Blown-down evergreens on the north shoulder are being superseded by birch and poplar. You swing south to the summit, where the trail ends, 0.75 mile from the A-Z Trail. A quiet lunch among Mount Tom's spruces and firs may reveal dark spruce grouse feeding toward you among the ferns and wood sorrel or pecking at the evergreen needles. The male sports a red eyebrow. In sunlight and shade his black and gray feathers hide him until he moves. This denizen of remote conifer forests is protected by New Hampshire law. His deliberate actions and lack of fear caused early hunters to think of domestic fowl and name him and his mate "fool hens."

After lunch, retrace your steps to the A-Z Trail and turn right. Follow it a short distance to the Willey Range Trail, which branches left toward Mount Field. (The A-Z Trail continues into the valley to join the Zealand Trail; thus its significance: Avalon to Zealand. For a description of the Zealand Trail see Hike 31.)

Through close growths of fir, spruce, and birch, you begin the 1 mile to Mount Field's summit. You emerge into more open woods and taller evergreens. Look behind you in the gaps between trees for views of Mount Tom. Keep on up the final pitch, passing the junction where the Avalon Trail descends, left. You reach the summit in another 100 yards. A small opening between dead or fallen spruce and fir affords a view south to Mount Carrigain and Carrigain Notch, also to Mount Hancock, North and South Twin, and more distant peaks, as well as the nearer Zealand Valley, westward.

To the north you walk across the trail and look over young evergreens toward the panorama of the summits south of Mount Washington— Eisenhower, Jackson, Webster, and Crawford Notch. Beyond Washington and its barren slopes below the

Spruce grouse

buildings and towers, Mount Jefferson looks more remote and unspoiled.

Return to the Avalon Trail for the descent. It drops sharply down the side of Mount Field through low spruces. Care should be taken here: the footing on broken stones, wet turf, and occasional mud is often treacherous despite the stone and log steps. The flat shoulder leaning toward Mount Avalon's rocks provides openings in the scrub for views north and east. Behind you Mount Field rises so abruptly, you'll understand why you descended so quickly.

The main trail bypasses the crest of Mount Avalon, but a side trail leads to the right a few yards up the rocks for a bird's-eye view of Crawford Notch and the hotel site 1500 feet below. Don't miss this lookoff because you are a bit weary. You'll see the highway parallel to the railroad winding through the notch, one of the great passes of the Northeast. Webster Cliff is a stark mass of sheer rock buttressing the mountain northward. In the distance you gaze at the long Presidential Range centered on Washington's barren cone, which you identify by the buildings and broadcasting towers.

Below Mount Avalon, the trail continues to drop rapidly down through the spruces to the junction with the A-Z Trail, and the return to Crawford Depot and your car.

43

Mount Starr King/ Mount Waumbek

Distance (round trip): 7½ miles
Walking time: 6 hours
Vertical rise: 2600 feet
Maps: USDA/FS 7½' Mt. Washington NW; USGS 7½' x 15' Pliny Range

A hiker in the White Mountains should see the Presidential Range from Mount Starr King. Thirteen miles northwest of Mount Washington across the upper valley of the Israel River, Starr King gives you a look at the complete panorama of the five rocky crests serrating the horizon eastward above the massed green slopes. From Mount Washington your eyes follow the skyline over Clay, Jefferson, Adams, and Madison.

In his 1859 book, the Reverend Thomas Starr King described the then-neglected views of the Presidentials from the north and northwest. He extols Jefferson "Hill," which he says "may without exaggeration be called the *ultima thule* of grandeur in the

artist's pilgrimage among the New Hampshire mountains, for at no other point can he see the White Hills themselves in such array and force." The Reverend King gives no account of climbing summits north of present US 2, but his name is fittingly given to the mountain that is the great lookoff for studying and enjoying the northern slopes of the Presidentials.

How to Get There
Parking and trailhead are in the village of Jefferson, north of US 2. Opposite the Waumbec Golf Club, 0.7 mile east of NH 116, you'll see a hiker sign and a Starr King Trail sign. If you approach from the east on US 2, it is 3.6 miles from NH 115. Turn up a narrow gravel road at the signs. Keep straight uphill, avoiding the right-branching driveways to several large houses. You enter the woods at a boundary sign for the national forest and soon emerge on the parking area.

The Trail
The Starr King Trail leaves the east end of the parking area on an old logging road, then turns left to join the old trail. You climb through hardwoods, paralleling the brook down

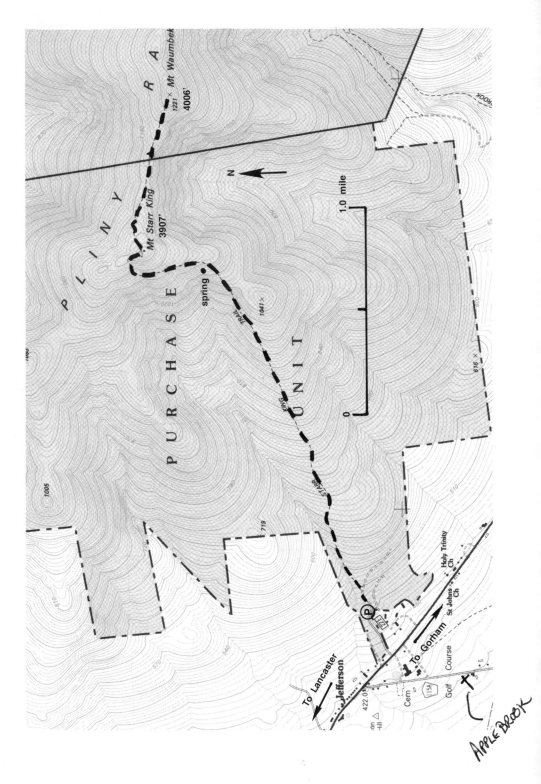

on your left. You pass the round foundation of an old spring house on the right and soon, at a sign saying SPRING, an old spring well up on the bank. The trail takes you up the mountain at an equable grade. As you climb into the zone of spruce and fir toward 3000 feet, you pass a spring on the trail's left slope. The trail swings around to the north as it continues up and up. It approaches the summit from that direction.

Spruce and fir screen views northward from the ledge. Proceed along the trail about 200 feet through the trees and emerge abruptly into a clearing. There before you—peak after peak—are the Presidentials!

Sunlight alternates with cloud shadows over the mountains. Often, mists gather around the rugged peaks of Mounts Adams and Washington. Binoculars bring out the Madison Hut at the col between Madison and Adams. You look into the depths of King Ravine on Adams. Watch for the train on the cog railway climbing Washington. Below your vantage point is the green valley of Israel River and Jefferson Meadows, and farther away you see wooded Cherry Mountain. The Franconia Range seems far away beyond numberless smaller mountains and ridges, but Lafayette's blue-green silhouette assures you that you're looking at Franconia Notch's giant. Your gaze inevitably returns to the main attraction, the Presidential Range.

When you finally look more to your left nearby, you notice a ridge eastward, where spruces rise to a wooded summit 1 mile away: Mount Waumbek, seemingly of no consequence. But a trail in that direction leaves from the southeast corner of the clearing below the site of the dismantled log shelter. It winds through the evergreens below the ridge, then ascends. Although roughly laid out among stumps and tree trunks, it is well worn by hikers adding another 4000-foot mountain for their records. Mount Waumbek is higher than Starr King—4005 feet against 3913.

Waumbek offers glimpses of the Presidentials through spruces at the end of a short trail past the summit sign on a tree. Clouds whirl turbulently overhead and gather around Mounts Adams and Madison. The appeal of Waumbek is primitive, a north-country wildness occasionally animated by small birds in the spruces—boreal chickadees and golden-crowned kinglets.

The Kilkenny Ridge Trail leaves the summit of Waumbek for South Pond 20 miles northeast.

Return to the clearing on Starr King for a final scanning of the panorama before you, then descend through woods brightened by the lowering sun along the trail you climbed when the day was new.

44

Mount Eisenhower

Distance (round trip): 6½ miles

Walking time: 5 hours

Vertical rise: 2725 feet

Maps: USDA/FS 7½' Stairs Mtn.; USGS 7½' Stairs Mtn.; USDA/FS 7½' Crawford Notch; USGS 7½' Crawford Notch; USDA/FS 7½' Mt. Washington SW; USGS 7½' x 15' Mt. Washington

Southwest from Mount Washington, rocky peaks extend toward Crawford Notch. One of these, Mount Eisenhower (formerly Mount Pleasant), commands a spectacular view to all points of the compass.

This broad dome overlooks sections of the famous 8-mile Crawford Path from Crawford Notch. Three beeline miles to the north, past Mount Franklin's long hump and Mount Monroe's two crests, Washington looms in its role as the highest point in the Northeast: it hosts tourists carried to the top by cog railway and automobile; it supports the summit buildings, towers, and observatory; it

tolerates—with occasional good weather—the many hikers on its exposed slopes.

Into the arctic-alpine world of Mount Eisenhower, the Edmands Path climbs up a west ridge and around the north base of the dome to the Crawford Path. There, near this junction, a side trail leads up the crags and over the rounded 4761-foot summit. On a clear day, from that vantage point high above the forests, the sky and rocks are elemental and clean.

How to Get There
To reach the Edmands Path, turn off US 302 at Fabyan onto the Base Road leading to the cog railway's base station. Soon Mount Eisenhower comes into sight as a hemispherical outline contrasting with its more jagged neighbors and identified by its above-treeline dome against the eastern sky. (The great cairn on the summit has flattened out in recent years. An easy way to identify Mount Eisenhower is to remember that it resembles Ike's bald pate.) Drive on the Base Road about 5 miles to an intersection. Turn right. You are now on the Mount Clinton Road. Drive 1.5 miles from the four corners. And drive carefully; there's

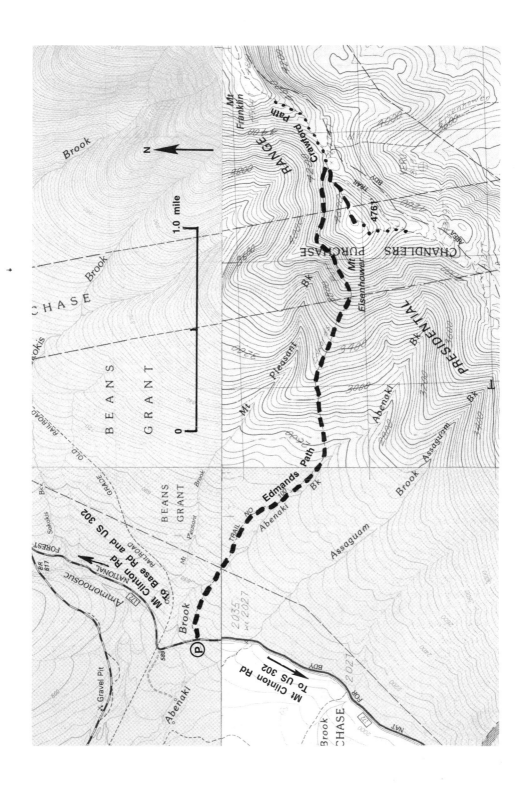

Mount Eisenhower

a startling 90-degree curve about 0.5 mile from the trail.

The Trail

In the parking area you'll see a sign for the Edmands Path. The great trail builder, J. Rayner Edmands, relocated and graded the path in 1909. It bears left among beech and yellow birch and crosses two small brooks on short footbridges. Then you'll cross Abenaki Brook. Keep to the right up an old logging road beside the brook. You begin to climb somewhat here. The trail swings left up the ridge that will take you to treeline. The grade steep-ens but is nowhere excessive. You enter spruce/fir woods, the habitat of the blackpoll warbler and Bicknell's thrush.

You climb up sections of graded fill held on the slope by rockwork. You notice rocks drilled and split with hand tools to clear and ease the way. In the upper spruce/fir woods the trail crosses three seasonal source-streams of Mount Pleasant Brook. Approaching treeline, you find the trail paved with flat stones. This improvement of Edmands's meticulous trail construction was a 1930s CCC task.

If a cloud thick as sea fog masks the

rocks, or if a storm threatens, heed the forest service warning sign in the last trees, and turn back.

Once above treeline, you will see that the Edmands Path splits into three gravel trails between ledges and across the alpine sward. Keep straight toward the junction with the Crawford Path. Then turn right onto the Mount Eisenhower Loop, a side trail over Mount Eisenhower whose rough dome rises ahead. (The Crawford Path bears left around the base.) You descend slightly and pass a little pool, Red Pond, on your left. Up the ragged ledges the trail zigzags, then takes you in a more gradual swing to the wide summit and the cairn. The green cushions all across the summit are the alpine plant diapensia. If you climb in mid-June, you'll see the array of white blossoms.

Be careful not to step on the plants as you walk around admiring the views.

Stepping stones are plentiful. To the north, up Mount Franklin curves the old and honored Crawford Path. Dropping away east of Mount Franklin, the ledges disappear into Oakes Gulf, where the Dry River (Mount Washington River) begins its turbulent run to the Saco River. Beyond Mount Franklin, you see a small peak on the left and a higher crest right, which combine to form Mount Monroe. Then comes Washington, often crowned by a misty cloud.

Your return follows the same route to the Edmands Path junction. Turn left down to the graded way and into the trees. The construction so carefully carried out by J. Rayner Edmands makes the descent as nearly painless as your tired legs will experience anywhere. But this ease may trick you: it's likely to lull you so that the descent seems longer than the climb.

45

Mount Crawford

Distance (round trip): 5 miles

Walking time: 4½ hours

Vertical rise: 2100 feet

Maps: USDA/FS 7½' Stairs Mtn.; USGS 7½' Stairs Mtn.; USDA/FS 7½' Bartlett

A rough oval of ledges around spruce scrub, Mount Crawford's 3129-foot promontory extends into the broad delta of ridges and valleys that flow 10 miles south from Mount Washington. Two great cliffs, 1.5 miles northeast, the Giant Stairs, identify Stairs Mountain and the long, forested Montalban Ridge. The Presidential Range's southern peaks appear at the far north end of the Dry River valley. To the northwest, Mount Willey looms over Crawford Notch.

A former bridle path, cut 15 years before the Civil War, passes east of Mount Crawford to Mount Washington. (A spur path rises to Mount Crawford's summit.) This route, called the Davis Path, was constructed by Nathaniel Davis, proprietor of the

Mount Crawford House, and brother-in-law of the famous Ethan Allen Crawford. Nathaniel Davis sold his horses about the time adventurous sightseers began riding up the Carriage Road being built from the Glen House in Pinkham Notch. After 1855 the bridle path fell into disuse and grew back to woods. In 1910, the AMC and volunteers reopened it, discovering, with the aid of a Maine woodsman, all the original path.

How to Get There
To make this historic and rewarding hike, drive about 6 miles west from Bartlett on US 302. Watch for a stone house known as Notchland Inn on the left above a railroad crossing for old US 302, now bypassed. You are at Notchland, which was once a station named Bemis, for the builder of the stone house. A short distance beyond this, you'll see a Davis Path sign on the right. Turn right into the large parking area.

The Trail
The Davis Path begins at the northwest corner along a rough roadway leading to the Bemis Bridge, a suspension footbridge over the shallow

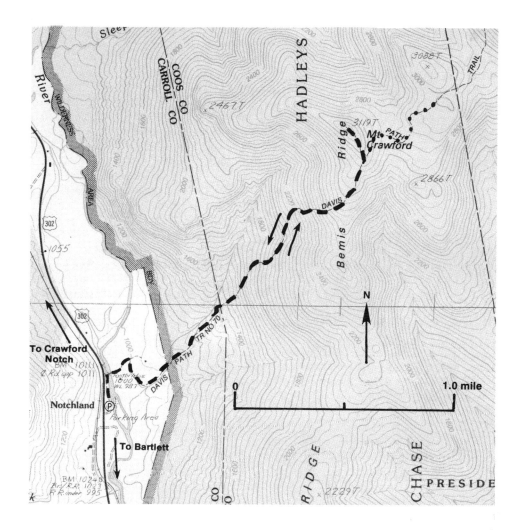

Saco River. Beyond the bridge you enter an open field. The trail keeps to the north edge adjacent to a wide lawn and house on your right. At a Davis Path sign follow a path into bushes and alders. It takes you to a pair of logs over a muddy brook channel. At the opposite bank, turn right. You'll walk through open woods and across a dry brook bed with smooth stones.

Soon you begin the climb along the old bridle path. The grade is steady, with occasional log or rock steps. You climb more steeply on straight stretches dug from the slope and supported on your left by rock retaining walls which Nathaniel Davis built for permanence. You wonder at the strong backs and patience of the men who worked with oxen, chains, and crowbars. The graded trail reminds you of the untold miles of New England's stone walls.

You follow winding turns as you approach the top of the ridge. You emerge from spruces on open ledges, where you look northwest to Crawford

Notch and Mount Willey. Keep right, over two wavelike swells and across an arm of spruce woods to rock again. Watch for cairns ahead and faded white and blue paint marks on the ledges among scattered spruces.

You come to a long slanting rock face. Signs indicate the Davis Path continuing to the right and the Mount Crawford spur ahead. Walk up that rock face.

At the top, the trail proceeds among ledges and spruces, marked by a few cairns and faded paint blazes. The trail stays on the ridge crest, and about 0.25 mile from the Davis Path you step out on the cliff that looks off to the Giant Stairs and the gravel slides of Montalban Ridge. Ledges continue around a small growth of spruces, with views up the Dry River—misnamed,

because it can be a turbulent, dangerous stream—to Mount Eisenhower, Mount Franklin, Mount Monroe, and Mount Washington. Walk around and look southwest to Mount Carrigain and its tower. To your left, down in the valley, you see the stone house and the highway. Mount Crawford gives you a complete 360-degree panorama for your 2.5-mile climb.

Giddy from mountain vistas, you may for a change turn to the tiny cranberry vines clinging to rock crevices along with alpine crowberry. Labrador tea and blueberries grow in the shelter of the 5-foot spruces. White-throated sparrows flit nearby. Cedar waxwings perch on dead twigs and survey the scene in their alert way. This is a place to linger, to look about again, and to eat a hearty lunch.

BACKPACKING HIKES

His pack was heavy but it made him feel free and secure because it contained shelter and food and everything they'd need in the woods. It was like carrying a home on your back.

—Daniel Doan
Amos Jackman

46

Mount Hancock

Time allowed: 2 days, 1 night

Distance (round trip): 9½ miles

Walking time (with pack for 5½ miles): 7½ hours

Vertical rise (including both peaks): 2400 feet

Maps: USDA/FS 7½' Mt. Osceola; USGS 7½' Mt. Osceola; USDA/FS 7½' Mt. Carrigain; USGS 7½' Mt. Carrigain

Your first overnight hike should test, but *gently*. It should give you the chance to try out new boots, pack, tent, cooking kit, and food—and, most important, your own capacity. But it should not include too many miles. The trip to Mount Hancock meets these specifications.

How to Get There
The Hancock Notch Trail goes north from the Kancamagus Highway at the hairpin turn about 10.5 miles east of Lincoln. Watch for a trail sign on the left. Just ahead on the right is parking at the Hancock Overlook.

The Trail
The trail follows a logging railroad grade through hardwoods merging with spruce and fir as you swing east above Hancock Branch's North Fork. The grade curves around the west shoulder of Mount Huntington at about the 2300-foot contour. In places, swampy ground nurtures lush sphagnum moss at either side of the packed fill. The rails have been gone since before World War I. Rows of blasted rocks still hold the fill in place. Cuts through ledge and banks are 10 and 12 feet deep. The fast, easy walking is interrupted at gullies and brooks once spanned by log bridges.

The hurricane of September 1938 laid down the trees that had begun to reforest the cut-over ridges and valleys. At the same time, Mount Hancock's north and east slopes were logged clear of all merchantable trees. For many years thereafter, the forest service closed off and kept watch over the area until the forest fire danger passed and new growth healed the devastation. The present trees demonstrate the rapid gains they make when protected.

The Hancock Notch Trail meets the Cedar Brook Trail branching left, northward, in spruce and balsam

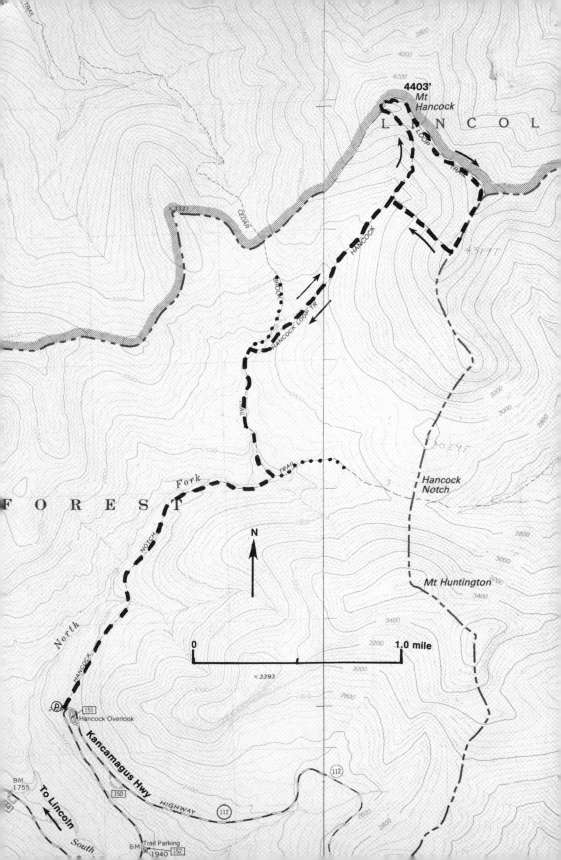

4403'
*Mt
Hancock*

L I N C O L

CEDAR

HANCOCK

HANCOCK LOOP TR

LOOP TRAIL

TRAIL

TRAIL

Fork

North

HANCOCK

NOTCH

*Hancock
Notch*

Mt Huntington

F O R E S T

N

0   1.0 mile

×3393

P
151
Hancock Overlook

Kancamagus Hwy

150   HIGHWAY   112

112

BM
1755

To Lincoln

South

BM   Trail Parking
1940   152

woods. You are 1.75 miles from the highway. (The Hancock Notch Trail continues east to the height-of-land and down to the Sawyer River, which drains into the Saco River south of Crawford Notch.)

Turn to the left across a little brook and begin the climb up the Cedar Brook Trail. The name derives from the brook on the far side of Mount Hitchcock, which is ahead and to your left, west of north. Mount Hancock is ahead and to the right, hidden like Hitchcock by trees. You are still following Hancock Branch's North Fork. You cross it five times in the next 0.75 mile. (To avoid crossings, there's a bushwhacked trail along the east bank.)

The brook takes on a rusty color. An old beaver pond, peat bogs, spruces, and tamaracks give the tan shade to the water. You follow the trail through a mossy bog where pitcher plants—those strange insect-eaters—grow near heavy turf interlaced with rootlets.

Watch on the right for the Hancock Loop Trail. It cuts into thicker woods as a wide aisle from the open, wet area, and soon takes you across the brook to an overused campsite of bare earth, stone campfire circles—and, after rain, mud. Don't bother to look for a place to pitch your tent. Seek your own site by continuing up the trail. It becomes a minor brook (sometimes dry) through jumbled rocks for a few yards. Next comes a boggy section. After 10 minutes from the overused campsite begin looking for your own private place.

I suggest as a landmark in a likely area the group of three big boulders to your left across the brook. You'll want to avoid two sites close to the water. Scout around above the big rocks or on the south side of the trail. You need only an opening large enough for your tent. Alternatively, you may climb farther up the trail as it rises above the brook and from there descend to level camping areas in the valley.

Along here you have carried your pack about 3 miles—far enough to have learned some packing tricks and trials, far enough to have felt, at least briefly, the exhilaration of carrying your home with you, the freedom of the backpacker.

The light nylon tent goes up quickly. Or it does if you've practiced in your backyard or even in your living room. Fluff out the sleeping bag. The traditional campfire may wait until you have cooked your meal on a backpacker's stove. Then a very small fire on bare ground warms and cheers as darkness approaches. It may also attract white-footed mice hopping delicately near. Later, when you're dropping off to sleep, they will rustle in the pack's food bags if you left them on the ground, and you will have to wriggle out of your bag to hang the pack in a tree by flashlight, bare feet cold in the dew.

To avoid this, take precautions earlier. After your meal you should always remember to hang food 10 feet up and 5 feet out on a tree limb to protect it from animals, particularly bears.

Next morning prepare for a day hike. Beyond your camp, the Hancock Loop Trail is still on the old logging road that parallels the valley on your left. The steady climb in young hardwoods and evergreens lifts you up to glimpses of the slide identifying Mount Hancock's south slope. It's a slippery-looking face of bedrock granite, at a distance smooth as gray glass above a jumble of rocks and gravel. Early ascents were made up the slide, a dangerous route now replaced by the wooded trail. You are now far above the brook. You come to the junction for the loop over Mount Hancock's

Mount Hancock

From the north peak summit, which you reach at an opening in the spruces, turn left to the head of the slide for a view toward the mountains around Waterville Valley, Mount Osceola, and some of the Sandwich Range.

Leaving the north peak summit, the trail descends along the crest of the ridge and turns southeast on a narrow winding traverse up and down, around blowdowns, and across surprising wet spots. The trail gradually ascends the south peak to its 4274 elevation. An opening a few yards east gives you an outlook over the Sawyer River valley.

Beyond the south peak, the trail turns right, west, and drops sharply away down through spruce/fir woods to the end of the logging road that returns you to the junction where you began the loop. Of the total distance around the loop, 2.5 miles, all but the ridge mile has been up or down as steeply as almost any trail in the mountains, which explains the 3 hours it requires.

Retracing your earlier steps to camp, you have time for another meal before folding up the tent and packing for the hike out. Douse your fire twice and stir the ashes—if you bothered with a fire. A backpacker's stove is faster and safer than cooking on a wood fire. Restore the site to its natural wildness, even to brushing up the duff flattened under your tent and sleeping mat, use a dead branch. And of course carry out all your trash.

For the return trip, 1.5 hours should be enough time—less, if you stride down the railroad grade like a veteran backpacker.

two summits. To your left the valley drops away to a gully and source of the brook—usually dry in summer—and to the base of the slide.

Both summits are more than 4000 feet high, yet wooded. To climb the 4403-foot north peak first—although the order chosen matters little—turn left down into the dry brook gully. The trail bears right, away from the slide's base, and enters the spruces. You climb up very steeply, but avoid the slide as the trail is cut up through the woods. Despite the angle, much larger spruces once grew here. You may still see remains of monster stubs and fallen trunks, some charred from forest fire.

47

Sandwich Mountain

Time allowed: 2 days, 1 night

Distance: 13 miles

Walking time: 9½ hours

Vertical rise: 2500 feet

Maps: USDA/FS 7½' Squam Mtn.; USGS 7½' Squam Mtn.; USDA/FS 7½' Waterville Valley; USGS 7½' Waterville Valley; USDA/FS 7½' Mt. Tripyramid; USDA/FS 7½' Center Sandwich; USGS 15' Mt. Chocorua

Viewed from a distance, the heavy silhouette that terminates the Sandwich Range's western reach contrasts with the much-photographed eastern pinnacle, Mount Chocorua. Sandwich Mountain rises massively from a broad foundation buttressed by ridges extending from Waterville Valley south to Beebe River and east to Flat Mountain Ponds. On the west, it slopes to Black Mountain above Sandwich Notch. Spruce/fir woods grow to the 3993-foot summit, but ledges offer partial outlooks. On this hike, the climb up Black Mountain from the west pro-

vides the spectacular views lacking on Sandwich Mountain.

First Day: Sandwich Notch Road to Sandwich Mountain to Black Mountain Pond

Distance: 7½ miles

Walking time: 6 hours

This big day of the trip includes all your climbing.

How to Get There
From Campton, drive east on the Waterville Valley Road (NH 49) about 3.5 miles to a right turn, south, onto the Sandwich Notch Road. Follow this narrow, steep, dirt road 3.8 miles to the Algonquin Trail, which begins on the left (northeast) side. If you are coming from the Center Sandwich end of the Sandwich Notch Road, turn at the Sandwich Notch sign in the village, drive along Grove Street, then bear left onto Diamond Ledge Road, which leads to the Sandwich Notch Road. The distance from the yellow blinking light in Center Sandwich to the Algonquin Trail is 7 miles.

Park off the road and shoulder your

pack. It should contain a tent; the shelter at Black Mountain Pond has been taken down.

The Trail

The Algonquin Trail, blazed yellow, follows a logging road almost 1 mile, crossing a brook, then branches left up toward the south face of Black Mountain. Climbing steadily among birches and beeches, it levels along the first bare rock and heath-like openings. Beyond a little seasonal brook you climb again abruptly to a col between a rocky knoll on your left and the main mountain ahead to the right. The next several pitches are difficult sections for the backpacker. In the evergreens you'll face one mass of creviced bedrock where you may decide to take off packs and pass them up.

The reward for this climb is a rocky lookoff into Sandwich Notch. The Sandwich Notch Road has been in use from the early days of settlement and once was bordered by farms and houses. From this viewpoint the trail turns back into thicker evergreens, then open rock with scrub growth here and there on the ridge leading to the summit.

The Algonquin Trail continues to a junction with the Black Mountain Pond Trail coming in from the right. The pond is your destination for the night, so you will return to this junction, from which you now have a 1.7-mile spur that will take you over Black Mountain and up Sandwich Mountain. (Note: if you are getting tired or the hour is getting late, save Sandwich Mountain for another day and go directly down the Black Mountain Pond Trail.)

Continue east on the Algonquin Trail. It crosses a ledge from which you look down at Black Mountain Pond 1000 feet below. Swinging somewhat left and entering spruces, you climb to Black Mountain's summit. Sometimes

moose spend a winter on Black Mountain. Watching the trail, and startled by droppings apparently left by a pony herd, you may not at first realize you're walking through a moose "yard." So dense are the spruce and fir trees that moose find winter quarters under the protecting branches and food from the evergreen tips. Snow, crusting upper boughs, roofs a sheltered stable for the huge animals.

The Algonquin Trail now descends to the ridge that leads to Sandwich Mountain. You pass occasional ledges and outlooks north, but mostly you ascend through spruce/fir woods. The Algonquin Trail joins the Sandwich Mountain Trail for the last few yards to the summit. (The Sandwich Mountain Trail comes in, left, from the Waterville Valley Road.) The spruces hide much of the view, but from rocks at the summit you get a lookout over Waterville Valley to Mount Tecumseh's ski slopes and Mount Osceola.

Retrace your route via the Algonquin Trail to the junction with the Black Mountain Pond Trail. Turn left (south) for the descent to the pond. The way is steep. Watch your footing and dig your heels in when gravity begins to get the best of you. The ledges and evergreens seem about to slide into the valley, yet they will probably stay in place. The tops of lower trees are on your eye level; you may have a close introduction to tiny golden-crowned kinglets. Approaching the base of this precipitous mountainside you descend through spruce woods that have never been cut. The trail levels out at beaver dams on the inlet to Black Mountain Pond. The trail swings around the west shore of the 6-acre pond, which is 32 feet deep, clear, and the home of speckled trout. But don't count on a fish dinner.

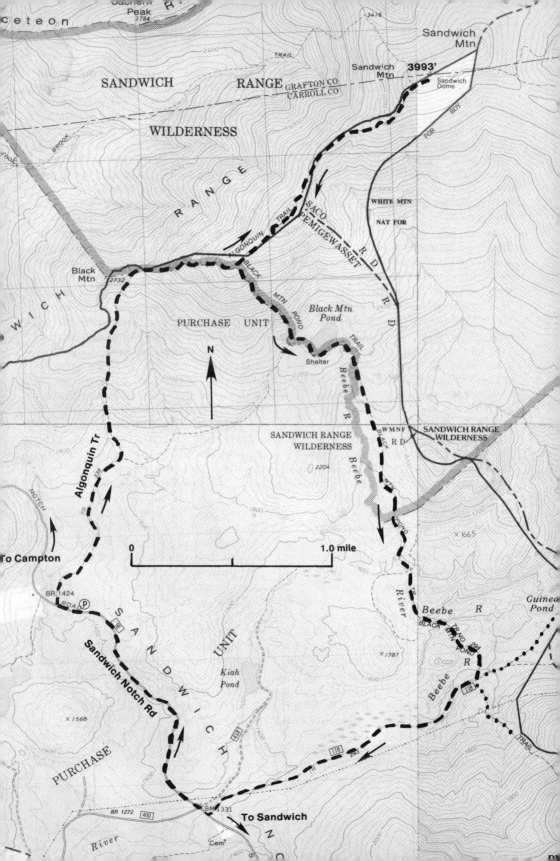

Second Day: Black Mountain Pond to Sandwich Notch Road

Distance: 5½ miles

Walking time: 3½ hours

Easy walking this day leaves you free to swim and lie in the sun all morning. The pond is a gathering spot for birds and animals. Kingfishers, cedar waxwings, blackbirds, and ducks may be seen. In the spruces, white-throated sparrows flit about, and red squirrels scold.

You look back up the steep slope you came down and feel pleased that you don't have to climb it.

After lunch, pack shouldered once more, you follow the Black Mountain Pond Trail above the south shore. The trail descends, crosses the outlet brook below rocks, turns right, and keeps to the east bank of the brook on a downhill slant along an old logging road. After about a half hour the trail crosses some low, wet ground partly spanned with bog bridges. You pass a small beaver pond on your right. Relocated around this beaver activity, the trail again descends gradually. The stream—still the outlet of Black Mountain Pond—flows into an extensive beaver pond of still water, dead trees, and a high and interesting dam. At the outlet, you step across and turn sharp left, following the yellow blazes downstream to rejoin the logging road. Turn right and continue until another bypass, left, takes you around more boggy ground. This rough trail leads you to the crossing of the Beebe River, here a brook. On the far side, after a short distance, the Black Mountain Pond Trail ends at the Guinea Pond Trail. Turn right on the Guinea Pond Trail for the Sandwich Notch Road. The Mead Trail, straight ahead at this junction, leads south up Mount Israel.

A shaded avenue, the Guinea Pond Trail follows the grade of a former logging railroad. It quickly bears left onto a detour path. Depending on the season and beavers, there may be flooding in this open country of swamps and dams. The swamp on your right is also a thicket of typical bushes, such as withe rod and black alder. You pass a gate. The grade runs below a power line. You descend to another gate, and you've reached the Sandwich Notch Road. Turn right (north) over the bridge across the Beebe River. Follow the dirt road north about 1.5 miles to the beginning of the Algonquin Trail and your car.

Sandwich Mountain Backpack

RUTH DOAN MACDOUGALL

48

East Branch Region/ Mount Carrigain

Time allowed: 3 days, 2 nights

Distance (round trip): 28 miles

Walking time: 21 hours

Vertical rise: 3300 feet

Maps: USDA/FS 7½' Mt. Carrigain;
USGS 7½' Mt. Carrigain; USDA/FS
7½' South Twin Mtn.; USGS 7½'
South Twin Mtn.; USDA/FS 7½' Mt.
Osceola; USGS 7½' Mt. Osceola;
USDA/FS 7½' Crawford Notch;
USGS 7½' Crawford Notch

A 3-day weekend is ideal for this hike. You exchange your daily routine in the modern world for life in the remote Pemigewasset Wilderness between Crawford Notch and the Franconia Range. The pleasures of distant woods and high mountains, as well as the satisfaction of backpacking and hiking nearly 30 miles in 3 days, may escape you unless you've walked enough to toughen your legs.

On the morning after the first day's 7-mile hike through Carrigain Notch, you'll want to rise from your sleeping bag eager for 13 miles exploring the trails to Shoal Pond and Thoreau Falls. And you'll really enjoy the trip if your legs still have plenty of spring in them for the third day's climb up 4680-foot Mount Carrigain.

For each of the 3 days, there are unique experiences to anticipate. First, Carrigain Notch, a true hikers' pass between mountain and cliff, opens to the headwaters of the Pemigewasset River's East Branch, where you camp at the site of the Desolation Shelter, which has been taken down. Second, in those secluded valleys you find miles of first-class walking because old logging railroads provide easy grades beside clear streams. Third, Mount Carrigain's summit surprises you as a triangulation point for the great ranges, and the splendid panorama draws all the mountains together into a coherent pattern.

Mount Carrigain's tower on the third day is the hike's culmination before you descend to your car and to civilization.

First Day: Carrigain Notch and the former Desolation Shelter

Distance: 7 miles

Walking time: 6 hours

How to Get There

You start your trip with a backpack into the wilds through Carrigain Notch. Drive west about 4 miles from Bartlett on US 302. Cross the bridge over the Sawyer River and turn left onto the Sawyer River Road. There's a large parking lot on the left across from the start of the Signal Ridge Trail, which serves as a way to the Carrigain Notch Trail.

Note: Because of past washouts, the Sawyer River Road may be closed to traffic. If it is, you'll hike an extra 2 miles from US 302 to the Signal Ridge Trail. Parking is available on the left of the entrance to Sawyer River Road. To find out the current situation, check at the Saco Ranger Station on the Kancamagus Highway in Conway (603-447-5448).

The Trail

Shouldering your pack, you climb up the Signal Ridge Trail by a logging road across Whiteface Brook, which pours through its little valley on your right as you climb the first ridge. The trail swings west away from the stream, and you enter a logged area. Avoid the side roads. After 1 hour or so from the car, you approach Carrigain Brook. The Carrigain Notch Trail forks right. The Signal Ridge Trail bears left. Turn right onto the Carrigain Notch Trail. (On the third afternoon you'll descend Signal Ridge Trail from Mount Carrigain's summit to this junction.)

Now you head north along the Carrigain Notch Trail and soon cross Carrigain Brook. The trail leads toward Vose Spur, which is ahead and to your left but mostly out of sight above the hardwood forest. The trail's easy route stays a considerable distance west of the brook. Two bypasses on your right approach the brook to avoid two beaver ponds on tributaries. Under Vose Spur your boots will teeter over rounded cobblestones of several dry washes from the mountainside—incongruous under the big trees but indicative of spring freshets.

At the base of the notch a clearing opened by a former beaver pond gives a view of the notch's cliffs. Keep to the left along a bypass around the debris left by the beavers. It takes you to the steep climb among spruces and birches to the pass at an elevation of 2639 feet. You are entering the Pemigewasset Wilderness.

Wild and unknown to many travelers, Carrigain Notch forms a gateway to the East Branch valley. On your left, a towering shoulder, Vose Spur, separates you from Mount Carrigain's main bulk. On the right, Mount Lowell rises above the cliffs that complete the gunsight formation of the notch. The trail crosses beneath these heights among rocks and young spruces.

Dropping down over rocks and roots but more gradual than on the south slopes, the trail winds to an old logging road, which you can identify by rocks blasted into star shapes. The woods remain predominantly evergreens. You cross Notch Brook near its source and discover yet another bypass trail off to the left of the logging road's boggy sections. Your westerly direction is taking you north of Mount Carrigain and south of Notch

Brook, until you descend to a railroad embankment and a junction with the Nancy Pond Trail joining from the right. (The Nancy Pond Trail comes from Crawford Notch and US 302.)

Turn left for the continuation of the Carrigain Notch Trail along the railroad grade. For a mile you walk through evergreens, which open up at the site of vanished Camp 20 and a trail junction. The Carrigain Notch Trail turns abruptly right, downhill. Straight ahead and across a brook, the Desolation Trail begins. Its name refers to the devastation once caused by logging. (From this junction on the third day, you'll climb the Desolation Trail to Mount Carrigain's summit.)

Your first day's hike is almost complete, and you may rest or explore here at old Camp 20. It's typical of many deserted East Branch logging sites that have returned to woods. Built by J.E. Henry and Sons Company of Lincoln, this Camp 20 remains only as rotted boards grown over by raspberry bushes. A dump hidden under forest duff contains rusty tin cans, old peavey ferrules, sled runners, and pieces of cast-iron stoves. In 1912 the clearing was alive with hustling men and horses working in the woods from daylight until dark. Trains carried away the logs. Now, most hikers scarcely pause in walking by.

One hiker did. He tells of discovering evidence of toil and poverty. Near the dump he unearthed a rotted leather boot that had been resoled four times. Nails held leather to leather on this relic, and attested to a lumberjack's "making do" his only pair of boots. Yet the hiker recalled that many old lumberjacks look back upon their younger days in the camps and forests as the best years of their lives. (Rough on the forests, however.)

Turn right at Camp 20 as the Carrigain Notch Trail heads toward the former Desolation Shelter 0.25 mile away, where you'll be spending the night. Situated among spruces, which provided its three log walls, the shelter opened toward a fireplace of rocks and a clearing above a boulder-strewn brook of transparent water—Carrigain Branch.

The water, however, may not be as pure as it looks because one of its sources is Carrigain Pond. You've heard about the unfortunate exchange between humans and beavers—*Giardia lamblia*. (See Introduction.) For your drinking water, walk back up the trail and watch for the tributary on the left, north, of its union with Carrigain Branch coming down from the south. This is the same brook you saw at Camp 20 and the beginning of the Desolation Trail. Filter or treat the water.

Because of bear activity in the Desolation region in the last several years, use extra care about hanging food and cleaning up after cooking.

Second Day: Loop to Stillwater Junction, Shoal Pond, Thoreau Falls, East Branch, and back to the former Desolation Shelter

Distance: 13¾ miles

Walking time: 8½ hours

This walk along railroad grades and old haul roads benefits from an early start, which lengthens the day. Besides, as the sun begins to rise, you walk along the trail through cool woods; leaves and grass shine with dew, and the birds are singing.

For this loop you should leave your overnight equipment at your tent site. Set aside lunch, water, rain gear, extra shirt—your usual necessities for a day hike—in a little pack or fanny

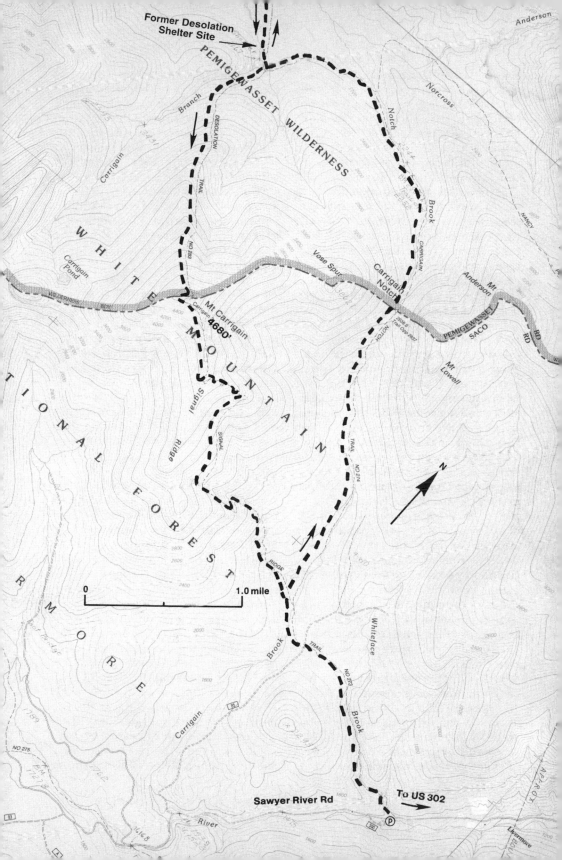

Former Desolation
Shelter Site

PEMIGEWASSET WILDERNESS

Anderson

Norcross

Branch

DESOLATION

TRAIL

NO 363

Carrigain

WHITE

Carrigain
Pond

WILDERNESS
BDY.

Notch

CARRIGAIN

Brook

Vose Spur

Carrigain Notch

Mt Carrigain
4680'

Carrigain

Mt Carrigain

MOUNTAIN

Signal

Signal
Ridge

SIGNAL

NO 275

TIONAL FOREST

RMORE

RIDGE

Brook

Carrigain

NO 93

Sawyer River Rd

River

Mt
Anderson

Carrigain Notch

Trail Opp 287

PEMIGEWASSET

Mt
Lowell

NOTCH

TRAIL

NO 274

SACO

RD

N

Whiteface

TRAIL

NO 273

Brook

To US 302

P

0   1.0 mile

pack. Place all remaining food in a strong bag and hang it out of reach on a tree. Without your overnight equipment, of course, you also leave behind your backpacker's freedom. You might want to camp somewhere along the loop. If you decide to do this, evaluate the additional weight, and the mileage to complete the loop on the third day in distance and time, which I've not included. Mount Carrigain from the west is STEEP! You may want to stay another day if you treat the loop as a backpack, instead of as a day hike.

From the former Desolation Shelter the Carrigain Notch Trail goes 0.5 mile down to its end at Stillwater Junction. Here you will find three trails joining. On your right, north, the Shoal Pond Trail leads at once across Anderson Brook. It will be your route for the morning. On your left, south, the Wilderness Trail begins as a curving bypass of the railroad grade, which lies straight ahead, thus avoiding two river crossings once spanned by trestles, but now difficult if not impossible. (The Wilderness Trail then parallels the East Branch below Stillwater, on or above the south bank. It will be your afternoon's return route back to Stillwater Junction.)

Now from the spruces at Stillwater Junction you take the north route, the Shoal Pond Trail, across the brook, aided by the concrete of a former dam. On the far side turn left on the railroad grade for a few yards, then follow the blue blazes to the grade that takes you straight for 0.5 mile through the new forest of poplar, wild cherry, white birch, yellow birch, and maple to the first crossing of Shoal Pond Brook. This is one of several bridgeless crossings in the 3.5 miles to Shoal Pond.

During logging days before World War I, standard-gauge steam locomotives chugged along the steel rails and crossties, that were later taken up, rotted, or burned. The stocky, tough little locomotives towed flatcars from Lincoln with men and supplies for the camps, and, when necessary as the trees were cut back, moved the camps themselves. The trains also carried Sunday excursionists, for a fee, and trout fishermen. The work trains returned to Lincoln piled high with spruce logs from landings along the East Branch and such tributaries as Shoal Pond Brook.

The Shoal Pond Trail takes advantage of one of these landings near the site of Camp 21. These platforms stored logs for the trains and were manned by a gang of men wielding peaveys. A cribbing of tree trunks supported J.E. Henry's landings against a slope above the railroad. The cribbing held the level rollway above the tracks where the flatcars waited. Horse teams dragged the sled loads from the haul roads to the landing and rested while peavey men rolled the logs off. Then the teamsters drove their horses back to the cutting woods. As many as 10,000 board feet of logs could be stored and rolled onto the flatcars below the landing. On the downgrade to the Lincoln sawmills, the flatcars shoved against the little engine. Brakemen scrambled over the slippery logs to primitive hand brakes. Link-and-pin couplings rattled, wheels clacked on rail joints, the engine chugged and thumped as it held back and blew out clouds of steam and smoke as well as sparks that often set the woods afire.

The scene now at the site of Camp 21 is quiet and verdant. Only worn sled runners protruding from the leaves on the ground, and cans from a dump, show that the camp ever existed. To the right in the brook a large, shallow pool collects water flowing

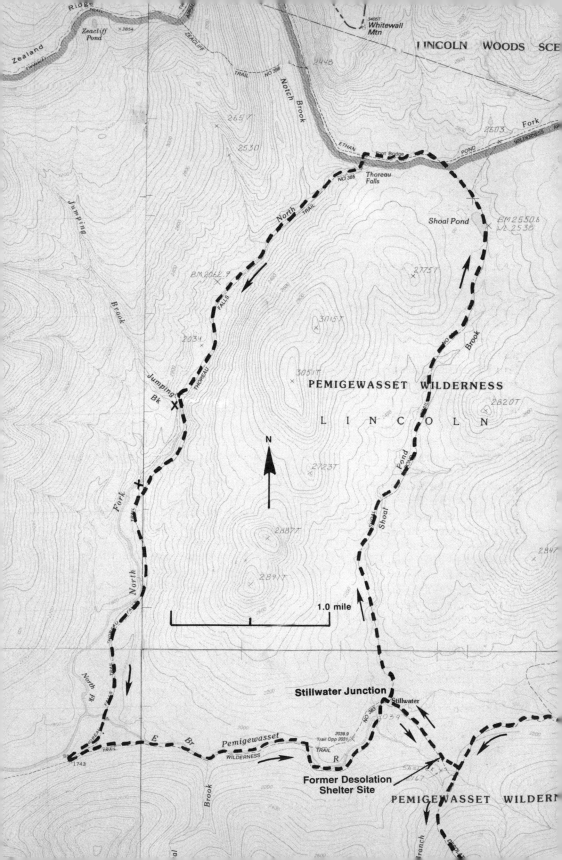

over nearly level ledge. Upstream the railroad grade ends, and you cross to the east bank. You follow old sled roads over log corduroy or often on modern trail walkways of split logs. The Shoal Pond Trail has been taking you through the eastern section of the Pemigewasset Wilderness.

A young forest grows on the earth scorched by logging and fire. You walk in the shade of innumerable trees. Under national forest protection since the early 1930s, this East Branch country has made a miraculous recovery. The wonder of returning forest speaks loud and clear for conservation, yet might suggest to the thoughtful hiker that earth and nature have given man more reprieves than he deserves.

Crossing to the west bank of the brook, you are approaching the pond through evergreens. The trail curves eastward again into more open country. Corduroy logs have been preserved by the cold and acid bog water. The land rises to dry ground. Midway on the east of the pond shore you can walk from the spruces to the water's edge, for a view of Whitewall Mountain and Zeacliff, north. Not much of Mount Bond is visible anymore.

A few hundred yards beyond the pond, the trail splits. Both forks lead to the Ethan Pond Trail. Take the left fork, which follows the old Zealand Notch railroad grade. This was another J.E. Henry enterprise that ended with fierce fires in 1886. Burned to bedrock, Whitewall Mountain north of you stands as testimony to the blazing inferno.

About 0.75 mile from Shoal Pond, you reach the Ethan Pond Trail, where the Shoal Pond Trail ends. Keep left onto the Ethan Pond Trail.

For the purpose of this hike, the Ethan Pond Trail provides a 0.5-mile transfer to the Thoreau Falls Trail.

(The Ethan Pond Trail comes from US 302 in Crawford Notch.) You follow the Ethan Pond Trail along the railroad grade to a footbridge over the East Branch's North Fork. Next, after about 0.25 mile, you come to the Thoreau Falls Trail on your left. This is your 5-mile return route south along the North Fork into the East Branch valley. (The Ethan Pond Trail goes north through Zealand Notch to the Zealand Trail near the AMC's Zealand Falls Hut.)

Take the Thoreau Falls Trail, left. You are in a Forest Protection Area: no camping or fires. Soon you see the need—bare ground, scattered trees growing through compacted earth. But the spruce forest will in time recover from too many campers. Descending to the ledges and the brook, you find an ideal lunch spot. Thoreau Falls and noontime come together if the day's hike is proceeding on schedule. The North Fork cascades down the slanting rock into a deep ravine. Named, of course, for the author of *Walden,* the white water glints in the sun and is visible to hikers on the western ridge, where Mount Bond, the highest summit in the area at 4698 feet, extends north to Mount Guyot, and Zealand Ridge curves along the northern horizon to Zeacliff.

After lunch you will have 7.5 miles of afternoon walking back to the former Desolation Shelter. The Thoreau Falls Trail continues from the steep bank beyond the head of the cascade. Care and caution are required due to slippery rock. Sometimes the flow of water will force you to retreat upstream in search of a less dangerous crossing.

Once on the far side you climb the bank, then pick your way down a precipitous, muddy, rooty drop as the trail descends into the ravine. The

Signal Ridge, Mount Carrigain

trail remains rough along the east side of the valley until you come to the sled road used by J.E. Henry and Sons' loggers when they began cutting the first-growth spruce in 1916. The trail improves as the valley opens out, and notably so when it meets the end of the old railroad grade and follows it.

This easy walking lasts about 2 miles. Watch on the left for the former highwater bypass. It is now the main trail and avoids difficult stream crossings. If you follow the grade to the North Fork you have gone too far by about 200 yards. The trail climbs the steep east slope. Its difficulty is preferable to negotiating (if possible) North Fork, Jumping Brook, and North Fork a second time to regain the grade.

Historically, this is an interesting area. The forest has reclaimed the old loggers' camps and railroad trestles. On the west bank below Jumping Brook there is a memorial plaque commemorating the deaths of Dr. Miller and Dr. Quinn of Hanover after a plane crash in February 1959.

The trail, ascending above an old landslide, swings south—parallel to the North Fork, but high up—before taking you down to the railroad grade once again. Turn left onto it.

Now you're all set for an hour's easy walking to the East Branch and a footbridge laid on 60-foot logs. (Eventually this bridge may be removed to conform to Wilderness status.) Beyond this crossing you'll think the trail is leading you away from your correct eastern, upstream direction back to the former Desolation Shelter. It is. The trail follows the railroad grade for almost 0.5 mile southwesterly to meet the Wilderness Trail. Stay alert for this junction.

Turn sharp left onto the Wilderness Trail. The slope is gradual, yet seems steep for an engine with cars behind it. After about 15 minutes the trail leaves the grade to stay on the south bank instead of crossing as the railroad once did. This bypass winds along the bank and through Crystal Brook, then down to the grade, which has returned to the south near the clearing at the site of Camp 18. Past the field of grass and fireweed some distance south of the East Branch, the trail stays on the grade as far as the riverbank where the railroad crossed. You need not. A more recent section of the Wilderness Trail takes you around two former difficult crossings. Stay on the grade to its end and step into the woods by this trail. It curves to the south of Stillwater, crosses Carrigain Branch, and returns you to Stillwater Junction for the completion of your day's loop. Turn to the right onto the Carrigain Notch Trail and retrace your morning walk to your tent site.

Third Day: Mount Carrigain via Desolation Trail and Signal Ridge Trail

Distance: 7½ miles

Walking time: 6½ hours

If the weather is fair on this day of the climb up Mount Carrigain, you are in luck. If clouds and rain have descended, I suggest you go back to your car through Carrigain Notch and save the mountain for a clear day. You can see the summit from the brook bed above the shelter site. Take a look and make your decision.

Shoulder your pack and walk up the Carrigain Notch Trail to the corner and junction at the site of Camp 20. Blue sky and sun overhead, turn right and you're on the way to Carrigain's summit on the Desolation Trail. (Clouds and rain up there, turn left on Carrigain Notch Trail.) Step across the brook. This is the last water.

You begin to walk on your trip's final railroad grade. It was a short spur track from Camp 20 to a landing at the base of the mountain. The Desolation Trail leaves it and heads up steeply before the embankment that appears to have been the landing and main sled road from the area around Carrigain Pond. Thereafter, the trail follows and crosses up between connecting logging roads as you surmount the ridge.

These former roads have thick bands of trees growing along them. Seen from a distance in the East Branch valley or from heights such as Mount Bond, they look like encircling, heavier-green, contour lines in the second-growth forest. Known to loggers as "dugway roads," these were literally dug into the mountainside to support heavy sled loads in winter when teams hauled logs down to the railroad landings. The highest roads of J.E. Henry's operations were winter tracks using brush and side logs as "bunters" to keep the lighter sled loads from slipping off the steep slopes.

The Desolation Trail takes you to the end of the uppermost road, where the steepest ascent begins. This angle stopped J.E. Henry's logging not because it was difficult but because it was unprofitable. Shrewd assessment of cost saved the present virgin forest bordering the Desolation Trail's top 0.5 mile to the summit. As a climber, you may also ponder the angle, but the slow upward pace will encourage you to enjoy the trees. The summit is 2 miles from Camp 20, wooded with low spruces, and overlooked by the tower, which is no longer a glassed fire lookout but a viewing platform above the evergreens for hikers.

The views on a clear day extend for miles in all directions. You can trace the route of your previous day's hike northwest of the summit. You look across the great country preserved in the Pemigewasset Wilderness. More distant mountains surround it. The Franconias rise on the horizon to the west, and the Presidentials northeast. Mount Hancock is a near neighbor on the southwest, while, southward, Tripyramid and the Sandwich Range complete the circle.

Now the time has come to descend to where you started on the first day. You have 5 miles to go and Signal Ridge will give you one more outlook.

The Signal Ridge Trail drops off the summit past the fire lookout's cabin site and well—which may have water in it, but treatment is necessary. The trail continues the steep descent to Signal Ridge. There you bear left along the crest for a fine view across Carrigain Notch to the cliffs on Mount Lowell. After abrupt downward progress, the trail slabs through a logged valley, passes Carrigain Notch Trail coming in left, and goes on down to the Sawyer River Road and your parked car.

49

Mount Isolation

Time allowed: 3 days, 2 nights

Distance (round trip): 14 miles

Walking time: 11 hours

Vertical rise: 3200 feet

Maps: USDA/FS 7½' Jackson; USGS 15' North Conway; USDA/FS 7½' Stairs Mtn.; USGS 7½' Stairs Mtn.

A high ridge to separate you from the highway, a long wooded valley with a clear stream, miles of white birches, and a remote, 4005-foot peak south of Mount Washington—these all appear for your enjoyment on your way to the summit of Mount Isolation. You follow the Rocky Branch Trail (named for the stream it follows, a tributary of the Saco River), the Isolation Trail, and the Davis Path on this woodsy 3-day hike. Because you return by the same route, you have the opportunity to see again the trees and brooks and views you passed hiking in; this double exposure reveals new secrets and discoveries.

Caution: This trip should be avoided in wet weather. Trails hold water, and the five crossings of Rocky Branch can be difficult or dangerous.

First Day: NH 16 to Rocky Branch and Isolation Trail

Distance: 3½ miles

Walking time: 3 hours

How to Get There

Drive north 5.5 miles on NH 16 from Jackson's covered bridge toward Pinkham Notch. Past a bridge over the Ellis River and beyond a White Mountain National Forest sign, right, turn left for the Rocky Branch Trail parking up an asphalt roadway. Here you adjust your pack. It should include a tent. The Rocky Branch Shelter Number 2 is scheduled to be removed. The Isolation Shelter has been taken down because it was in the Presidential Range–Dry River Wilderness.

The Trail

The Rocky Branch Trail begins at the north end of the parking area. It heads uphill and soon joins an old logging road angling left up the slope. This route, opened in 1933, was a CCC project. I recall the piles of brush left by the crews and the stumps from trees that had grown in after horse-logging days.

The trail takes you up west and north from the highway in a forest of beech and yellow birch. About 10 minutes from your car a ski touring trail joins, left, marked with blue blazes. Look behind you to make sure you don't take the ski touring trail when you return. It coincides with the Rocky Branch Trail for a few hundred yards, then bears right across a small stream. Keep to the left away from the logging road as your route zigzags up to another logging road and to switchbacks often root-tangled and rocky.

Rising steadily up this unremitting series of slopes for 2 miles, the trail approaches the spine of Rocky Branch Ridge, but there's wet footing ahead. A left corner, westward, takes you to another ancient logging road down a slight incline, which levels across an area of springs and two streams which form Miles Brook. The trail ascends again. Spruce/fir woods begin at this elevation near the 3000-foot sag in the main ridge, which attains 3660 feet at an unnamed summit to the right of the trail. Across a muddy height-of-land you can avoid some of the boot-churned bog by taking an unofficial bypass left through the evergreens, and back to the trail. It dries out somewhat as you come to a sign for the wilderness area you are about to enter—the Presidential Range–Dry River Wilderness. Beyond this sign, camping must be at least 200 feet from streams, trails, and former campsites.

Descending the ridge, the trail is sometimes a running rivulet. The rounded rocks, eroded from the thin soil as far back as the days when this was first a sled road, are hazards to your footing. Occasionally, through the trees, you can see across the Rocky Branch valley to Montalban Ridge, but there's difficulty in identifying summits along it, such as Mount Davis and Mount Isolation. The trail improves greatly when it crosses a trickle of water to the left and takes to a logging road dug from the slope. This eases your way down to Rocky Branch.

There's no footbridge to take you across to the Isolation Trail, which is your upstream hike for the second day. This crossing can be dangerous at high water. An alternative is to bushwhack upstream on the east bank to pick up the Isolation Trail after its first crossing, about 0.5 mile. In dry weather you can usually stay on the Rocky Branch Trail by stepping from rocks in the stream to a ledge above pools. Atop the bank beyond the ledge, the Isolation Trail begins on the right. Turn sharply left and follow the Rocky Branch Trail along the old railroad grade for 100 feet. The Rocky Branch Shelter No. 2 (or its site after removal) is in a little clearing above the stream. You may seek a campsite in the vicinity, but be sure it's 200 feet from the trail, stream, clearing, and any other obviously used camping place.

Second Day: Rocky Branch to Mount Isolation

Distance: 4½ miles

Walking time: 3½ hours

Your morning hike up Rocky Branch follows the Isolation Trail from the junction just north of the site of Rocky Branch Shelter No. 2. The trail turns left up from the railroad grade until, regaining the grade, it follows that route wherever possible, but avoiding slides and washouts. A forest of white birches has taken over the blueberry barrens of years ago. Under the birches, hobblebushes spread broad leaves that shade the fern fronds and the fanlike leaves of wild sarsaparilla. The valley has seen many changes: spruce logging, then the fires of 1914 and the scorched earth they brought, blueberry bushes, sprouting poplar and wild cherry growth, and now tall white birches where the old spruces grew.

The Isolation Trail goes up the valley of Rocky Branch for about 1.75 miles, with four crossings of the stream, two of which are only 100 yards apart. The old railroad trestles went up in flames or rotted away, so you must choose stones to step on or wade with a staff. Occasional sections of the trail keep to the side of the hill on the east bank for rough but somewhat drier footing above the stream. Large boulders here and there interrupt the flowing water and form pools below alder thickets. You walk in a long grove of white birches.

Beyond the final crossing to the west bank, the trail leads into spruces and over damp ground along a tributary brook. As the flow of water dwindles you should consider selecting a place for your tent. Although the tributary stream you're following can be said to have its source near the site of the former Isolation Shelter, this spring, which supplied hikers, has sometimes been dry. I suggest you set up your tent—of course 200 feet away from the trail and stream and in a spot never used by other hikers. And don't drink the water without boiling or other treatment.

Then continue up the Isolation Trail to the Davis Path. At this junction you have reached an elevation of about 3800 feet. Clear skies on this second day of your trip mean that you should keep on to Mount Isolation. You are only a mile from its summit off the Davis Path to the south. If clouds and rain envelop the junction, you may

very well postpone the remainder of your hike until morning and possible fair weather.

The Isolation Trail heads north, coinciding with the Davis Path for 0.25 mile before it forks west and descends to the Dry River Trail. The Davis Path extends between US 302 in Crawford Notch, 11 miles south, and Mount Washington, an extremely rugged, mostly exposed 4.5 miles. (For the section of the Path near US 302 see Hike 45, Mount Crawford.)

Take the Davis Path south. It soon passes the site of the Isolation Shelter. A brief description of the old log shelter will pay tribute to its solidity, its usefulness of 50 years since I first slept in it (and it was older than that), but more especially to its architecture. A log cabin with an open gable end facing the fireplace on a huge rock, it was a more comfortable shelter than the common Adirondack type with the overhanging front eaves. A campfire reflected back inside, both to the lower bunk and the upper bunk. Isolation Shelter never trapped smoke as do the open-fronts with low eaves. You never knocked yourself silly forgetting to duck as you went out. It always suggested to me a simpler and more primitive time in the mountains.

The trail climbs a spruce ridge overlooking Rocky Branch valley, left. But keep your eye on the trail. Watch for a spur trail right, at a small cairn and small sign. You scramble up a long 100 yards through spruce scrub to the flat, rocky summit of Mount Isolation.

The spruce scrub offers no obstacle to the outlook as you step across the ledges. The western horizon at once draws and holds your attention. The southern peaks of the Presidential Range begin in the south near Crawford Notch at Mount Jackson and extend north to Clinton, Eisenhower, Franklin,

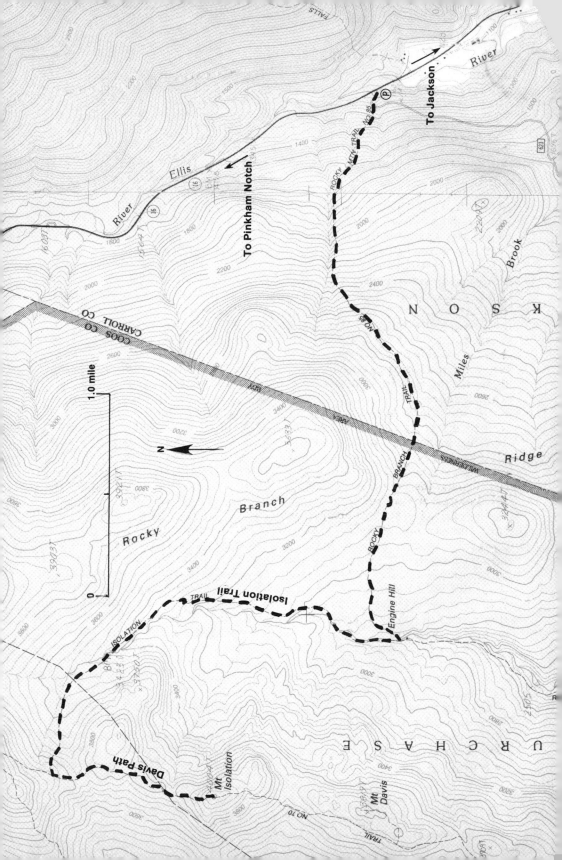

and Monroe, in a long serrated array to the great peak of Washington, which strikes into the sky 4 miles north of you. Mount Isolation places you high between two valleys that sweep down from Mount Washington to Crawford Notch; the line of summits, near whose northern end you stand, is named Montalban Ridge. You have hiked the valley to the east, Rocky Branch; to the west between you and the southern peaks, you look into Dry River valley, which isn't dry. Its upper waters are apparent as cascades on the headwall of Oakes Gulf between you and Mounts Monroe and Washington. (Dry River can quickly become a raging torrent. It bears another, more appropriate name: Mount Washington River.)

Mount Isolation is a grandstand seat for cloud shows. Often, white wisps and tumbling fogs swirl among the southern peaks. On some bright, clear days, storm clouds suddenly mass around Washington's cone and obscure the buildings and towers. If the storm threatens rain on Mount Isolation, retreat to your tent. Retrace your way east down the spur trail and turn left onto the Davis Path. The site of the former shelter is 20 minutes away. Turn right onto the Isolation Trail for the protection of the tent you've pitched away from the tributary to the Rocky Branch.

Third Day: Davis Path–Isolation Trail Junction to NH 16

Distance: 6 miles

Walking time: 4½ hours

Perhaps this morning brings clear skies after a previous rainy afternoon that kept you from Mount Isolation. You still have time to go up it, because this third day's hike is almost as moderate as the previous days'.

If you're early enough to Mount Isolation, you'll see the sunrise brightening Mount Washington, or maybe a shining white cloud around the peak. If rain pours down this morning, and you really want to reach the summit, you'll just have to slog along through the downpour. You'd be wiser to wait for another chance. There's nothing to see on Mount Isolation in a rainstorm except spruce scrub, ledges, Labrador tea, and mountain cranberry.

For the return hike, walk back down the Isolation Trail to Rocky Branch, and down the stream to the junction with the Rocky Branch Trail. Turn left onto the Rocky Branch Trail, cross the stream, and climb over the ridge. Then it's all downhill to NH 16 and your car—but avoid the ski touring trail, and turn right off the logging road just above the parking area.

50

The Mahoosuc Range

Time allowed: 7 days, 6 nights

Distance: 33 miles

Walking time: 32 hours

Vertical rise: 8600 feet*

Maps: USGS 7½' Berlin; USGS 7½' Shelburne; USGS 7½' Gilead (Me.); USGS 7½' Old Speck Mtn. (Me.)

For many years the Mahoosuc Range was little known except to the "through-hikers" of the Appalachian Trail, who said it was the toughest 30 miles between Maine and Georgia. Never a part of the White Mountain National Forest, this route is now federally protected as a segment of the Appalachian National Scenic Trail.

The town of Gorham and the Androscoggin River separate Mount Madison and Mount Moriah from the westernmost of the Mahoosucs, Mount

---

*This is an estimate based on map contour counting; the rises are frequent.

Hayes. The AT, descending from Mount Moriah south of the Androscoggin, crosses at Shelburne east of Gorham on US 2. The AT follows the Centennial Trail toward Mount Hayes for the first 3.75 miles of this 33-mile backpack over the summits of the range to Grafton Notch and ME 26 north of Newry, Maine. From Mount Hayes the AT follows the AMC's Mahoosuc Trail.

The distance as the crow flies is only 18 miles. Allowing for the walking distances to ascend and descend at the ends of the range, and a southerly swing and some zigzags from peak to peak, the extra miles are up and down along the range.

The varied worlds along the way include hardwood forests, mountain meadows, spruce-shaded slopes, subarctic barrens, frequent ledges, sharp ravines, and summit after summit. The Mahoosucs are a unique experience. Leisurely travel enhances the experience; the Mahoosucs deserve a week. Of the 7 days allotted, you hike 6 days with time to relax at intervals and still make camp long before dark. One day is a spare. Use it when a storm engulfs the range by taking refuge in a tent or in one of the four shelters. If your week's weather turns out to be perfect, you have a day to rest and loaf at Speck Pond shelter before completing the Mahoosuc Range on Old Speck Mountain and descending to Grafton Notch, where you meet asphalt again on ME 26.

Transportation arrangements will vary to fit individual plans. You can leave your car parked near the trail at Grafton Notch and be driven around west to Shelburne. You may plan to be met at Grafton Notch on the 7th day.

Although either Shelburne or Grafton Notch could be the starting point, the northeast direction from Mount Hayes has one specific advantage. Progress northeastward gives you an exciting sense of increasing wildness. With this you also enjoy a continual, although intermittent, ascent: Mount Hayes, 2555 feet; Mount Success, 3565 feet; Old Speck, 4180 feet; with 10 other summits in between.

The Mahoosuc Range has become a "laboratory" for AMC research on trail use and methods for preserving the mountain environment. First with the cooperation of the Brown Company, and more recently with the James River Company, the AMC has replaced old shelters, built tent platforms, and improved the trail with stone steps and stairs and log walkways as well as with waterbars for erosion control. (There is now a small fee for overnight stays at Speck Pond Campsite.) They have also installed boxes with cards at the trails' starts to check the number of hikers using them. It's a good program and needs your assistance—the cards take just a few minutes to fill out. Of course, carry out your trash, keep campsites clean, and help the caretaker when there is one. The plan of this backpack takes you

to shelters for 5 of the 6 nights. You will need your tent, however, at Trident Col Tent Site, and probably near the shelters if they are fully occupied when you arrive. Also, you may require the tent for protection in an emergency such as an injury or a severe storm. Otherwise, no camping is allowed except at authorized locations. Fires are allowed only at shelters and at Trident Col Tent Site. Backpacker stoves may be used along the trail for a hot meal, and are almost a necessity at the shelters if the fireplace is in use when you want to cook. And carry a collapsible water container for trips to the springs at some of the shelters.

Concerning your outfit, I will point out that it should be as light as possible, consistent with carrying plenty of food, water, and adequate equipment. Your tent, stove, cooking utensils, sleeping bag, rain gear, clothing, and the backpack itself *must* be tested and reliable. None of them can be replaced. If you are not an experienced backpacker, I suggest that you try out both equipment and similar food on at least two shakedown trips before going on this one. Two other admonitions occur to me. One necessity always in short supply along the summits of the Mahoosucs is water. Sources are few, far between, and except at shelters, often unreliable. You'll need more water bottles than for ordinary hikes. Next, fitness. Obviously, strength and endurance for heavy backpacking are absolutely necessary to insure both safety and enjoyment.

These comments about the demands that the Mahoosucs make on you and your outfit are meant not to discourage you but to advise on the measures you should take for a happy and rewarding backpack.

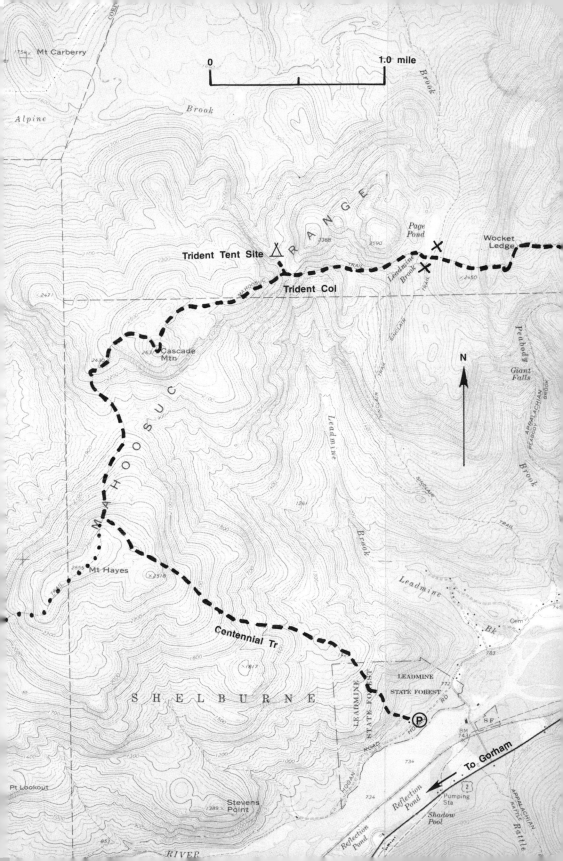

First Day: Hogan Road, Shelburne, to Mount Hayes, Cascade Mountain, and Trident Col Tent Site

Distance: 8 miles

Walking time: 6 hours

You'll want to be at this Shelburne trailhead early in the morning, perhaps from overnight accommodations nearby. The day's backpack will be long but not overly strenuous or rugged.

How to Get There
Drive US 2 to North Road in Shelburne. North Road's western junction with US 2 is 3.5 miles east of Gorham. (Parking for the Rattle River Trail, the route of the AT south, is about 300 yards farther east on US 2.) Turn north onto North Road and drive across the bridge over the Androscoggin River. At 0.5 mile from US 2, turn left onto Hogan Road. Drive this rough dirt road for 0.25 mile to your point of departure (parking overnight is not advised). The Centennial Trail begins on the north side of the road as a wide pathway remaining from former logging operations.

This is the last chance to check your equipment and food and water. Take an ample day's requirement of water. There may be none on the trail until Trident Col Tent Site.

The Trail
The Centennial Trail was named for the AMC's 100th anniversary, when it was laid out and cut in 1976. After 150 feet along the pathway, turn left at a sign where the woods road continues straight ahead. You are on a trail now. It winds up through a hardwood forest. The white AT blazes lead you upward over stone steps past ledges on the right to the first lookoff on the left, across the lake formed by a dam in the Androscoggin bisected by the Canadian National Railroad—the former Grand Trunk. Face around and follow a short section of trail north to an old logging road, which the Centennial follows to the left. Views and occasional steps alternate with easy slabbing of the contours as you walk through beech woods. Some of the gray, smooth trunks show marks of claws dug in by bears climbing eagerly for beechnuts. On several ledges you'll walk over the brass plugs that identify the Appalachian National Scenic Trail.

At last above a jumble of rock slabs you get the first glimpses of the Mahoosucs rising away ahead of you to the east. The trail curves up into open spaces among scrubby spruces to a bare knob, then on through birches to the junction among sparse evergreens at the Mahoosuc Trail from Mount Hayes and Gorham.

Here you may leave your pack and follow the Mahoosuc Trail west over the summit of Hayes to the cliffs above Gorham and the wide easterly bend of the Androscoggin south of the smoking paper mills of Berlin. Away west, Madison, Adams, and Washington rise magnificently stark and barren at the summits. You look south to Pinkham Notch and the Carter-Moriah Range forming the notch's eastern slope. This side jaunt over Hayes will take about 45 minutes, but is worth it on a clear day, and I've included the distance and time in the total.

Back at the junction with the Centennial Trail, shoulder your pack and head north on the Mahoosuc Trail, which is now the AT. It descends from the bare ledges, blueberry bushes, and evergreens of Mount Hayes into the leafy woods of the col between Hayes and Cascade Mountain. This col might better be described with the woodsman's term "sag" rather than the mountaineer's "col." It's a low wooded valley between the two mountains. Water may trickle below the lowest point of the sag into pools (if any) deep enough to give you water by the cupful.

Next comes Cascade Mountain. The beeches and yellow and white birches change to small, park-like maples, then to bushes and broken slabs of rock. From here you'll be treated to a special sunset show. The Androscoggin valley begins to close in with shadows. You stand far above and look across the Presidentials sharply etched by western sunlight. Move on along the ridge through spruce woods alternating with ledges and damp sphagnum moss. At the east shoulder, the Mahoosuc Trail drops steeply toward a view of distant peaks and ridges. The descent pushes your pack against your shoulders, and your hands seek steadying holds on bushes and trees, until the trail levels out at Trident Col. A spur trail leads left to water and four tent sites. This will be your camping place.

Second Day: Trident Col Tent Site to Gentian Pond Shelter

Distance: 5 miles

Walking time: 4 hours

The Mahoosuc Trail the next morning leads on eastward by an old logging road descending somewhat and slabbing south of middle Trident Peak. You cross trickles of water here and there through the hardwoods. The trail takes you up to a more recent, bulldozed road, which, after a short distance, bears right. The trail branches left, and you follow it among bushes and young trees up a gradual slope to a level section. The approach to Page Pond through tall grass shows you first the spruce ridge beyond, then the oval of water. In late summertime, closed gentians bloom near the beaver dam. Depending on the latest beaver work, the trail may cross over the dam's poles and mud.

An easy walk among spruces brings you to the base of the next height, Wocket Ledge, where the ridge rears up suddenly. You dig for footholds and test spruce roots and branches for secure hand grips. The ledge itself appears at the crest 50 yards to the left, about 0.75 mile from Page Pond. The climb has been strenuous, and you'll want to sit for a while and look off at the wild country near and far.

Back to the trail and up beyond the open ledge, you follow the trail in spruces. Descending, you pass a spring and the beginning of a Peabody Brook branch. Ascending and descending— the theme of the Mahoosucs—you slant down to a mountain pond called Dream Lake.

The trail turns left along the lake shore. By stepping quietly through bushes down to the water, perhaps you see a moose feeding, belly-deep in the lake. If only lily pads and quiet ripples meet your eyes, proceed along the trail and across the inlet to the northeast end. There the Peabody Brook Trail terminates at the Mahoosuc Trail. (The Peabody Brook Trail comes up from North Road in Shelburne off US 2.) A short walk down Peabody Brook Trail takes you to a striking camera shot across Dream Lake to Mount Washington.

Returning to the Mahoosuc Trail, you head east along the inlet brook.

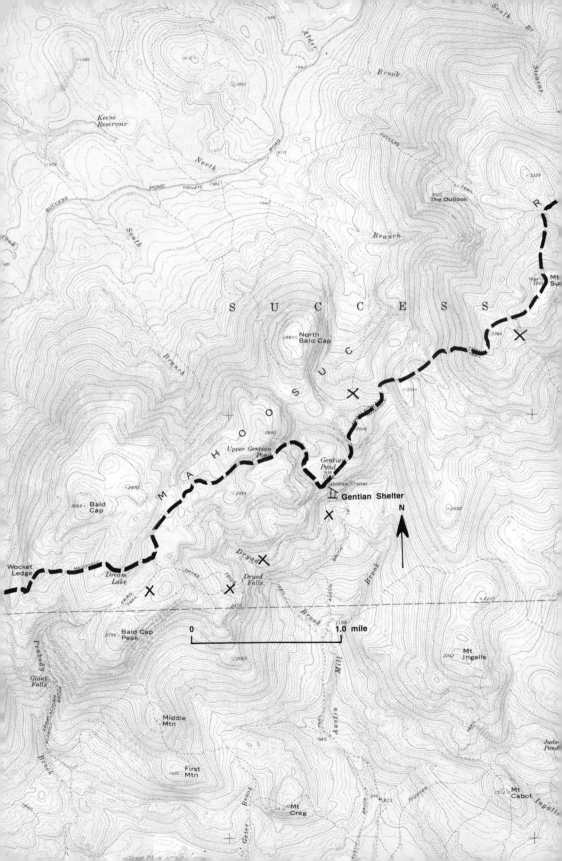

Keene
Reservoir

North
POND
PRIVATE
1581

ROAD
1610

Alder

Brook

South Br
Stearns

SUCCESS

TRAIL
3025
The Outlook

R
3335

Mt Su
Ingalls 3565

South

Branch

S   U   C   C   E   S   S
3364

North
Bald Cap
4927
S
U
2544
C
C
E
S
S

M
A
H
O
O
S
U
C
2850
2668
Upper Gentian
Pond
Gentian
Pond
BM
Gentian Shelter

2970
2755

⌂⌂ **Gentian Shelter**

N

3065 Bald
Cap
2402

Wocket
Ledge
Dream
Lake
Dryad
Dryad Falls
TRAIL
2226
TRAIL
DRYAD
Mill
Brook
Austin
Brook
3217

Bald Cap
Peak
2795

0   1.0 mile

1198

2000
Mt Ingalls
2242

Peabody
Falls
Giant
Falls
APPALACHIAN
TRAIL
Brook

Middle
Mtn

First
Mtn
1685

Mt
Crag

Gates
Brook
BM 823
SCUDDER
1512

Mt Cabot
Ingalls

Juds
Pond

The trail is damp, but log walkways offer dry footing. It swings left across a bog, again on walkways above the water, to a log ridge. The trail's up-and-down windings take you to a height-of-land so flat and swampy as to be almost imperceptible. The new watershed's first display appears at the boggy inlet to Moss Pond, formerly Upper Gentian Pond. You leave the shoreline for a rough, northern traverse back in the evergreens till you return to the pond near the outlet. There on your right you see a beaver dam so high that it seems barely to hold the brimming little basin from pouring down the mountainside. The dam has been doing this for many years. Two beaver lodges on the far shore house the caretakers.

The trail follows the outlet brook a short distance. Then as your way turns left, your attention will be occupied by the massive boulders it meanders among during the steep descent. A turn to the right leads you away from a cliff among white and yellow birches and swamp maples to Gentian Pond. The trail has been relocated from the west shore of Gentian Pond to its east shore; this eliminates a steep scramble down a ledge to a crossing of the outlet brook just below the shelter.

The shelter and its outside fireplace of piled stones rest on an abrupt, wooded dropoff, which falls away so steeply that you have a splendid view to the Androscoggin River far below in its wide valley. (From Gentian Pond Shelter, the Austin Brook Trail descends to Shelburne's North Pond. Your northeast backpack in the morning will take you beyond this last trail south from the Mahoosucs.)

The pond water is handy and serves well enough to rinse yourself. For drinking water you follow a faint path a good distance north among the shore spruces to an inlet trickling clear and cold past green sphagnum moss.

Third Day: Gentian Pond Shelter to Carlo Col Shelter

Distance: 5¾ miles

Walking time: 6½ hours

Mount Success is your big objective after breakfast at Gentian Pond Shelter. The climb measures the mountain's bulk rather than its height, which is a moderate 3565 feet. The up-and-down approach makes you think that the mountain has retreated beyond ridges to fortify itself against your attack.

In early morning, a steep climb places you on ledges above the pond. Then you descend and climb again over the first of two rugged little hills protruding from the mountainside. After the second knob, a little rivulet provides a canteen filling: no more certain water until the end of the day's hike at Carlo Col Shelter.

The trail continues, steep and difficult. You surmount blocks of granite, which obstruct the way and indicate an old slide. Then you cross a washout grown to brush, and begin to climb in the spruce/fir forest. The damp woods are the habitat of the deliberate spruce grouse. The trees dwindle to evergreen scrub at open ledges, and you climb toward the summit through more scrub and over bare rock.

Mount Success spreads before you northern vistas of lakes and wilderness as well as an unusual perspective toward the Presidentials. The summit itself presents the first muddy areas typical of high Mahoosuc ridges above treeline. Lying in hollows between rock

1579 1578 1579
VL 1569
Shelter
Brook
1534
x2162
OXFORD CO
COOS CO
1419
1622
PRIVATE 1435T
1674 CULV
1635 WL

R I L E Y
(TA 1)

Shelter Bk
NOTCH TRAIL
Mahoosuc Notch

Fulling M.
Mtn

South Peak

Full Goose She

North Peak

MAHOOSUC RANGE

M A H O O S U C

Goose Eye Mtn
Goose Eye Mtn

N

2441

Carlo Col Shelter
Carlo Col Shelter

2832

Mt Carlo

Carlo Col

R A N G E
BK
2972
OXFORD CO
COOS CO
A MAHOOSUC

0   1.0 mile

2508

2275x Jakes
Notch

faces, the black earth has a dry crust in hot weather. Stay on the split-log walkways or you'll be into ankle-deep muck. Various heath plants border this rich humus. Matted dwarf spruces testify to the severe winds.

From Mount Success, the Mahoosuc Trail turns left down a barren shoulder into scrub and taller evergreens. The trail is rocky and at times closed in by luxuriant spruce/fir branches. Several boggy areas can be extremely wet after rain. You level out and descend into a col and junction with the Success Trail on your left. (The Success Trail is the first of five trails from the Mahoosuc Trail to the Success Pond Road, here 3 miles north. This paper company road runs northeast 14 miles from Berlin to the pond.)

For the next 1.25 miles, the Mahoosuc Trail follows a northeast ridge. You climb and slab wooded contours, then descend, only to climb and descend again. In a little hollow an AT sign marks the New Hampshire–Maine line. After some rugged climbing, the trail takes you to a north outlook on bare rock surrounded by scrub and Labrador tea bushes. The view is across the vast north country.

Now the final climb down this ledge to Carlo Col gives any backpacker pause for thought. You may wisely decide to take off your pack and lower it to a companion who has made his way down, packless, by clinging to spruces and gripping with both hands on fingerholds of rock while groping for footholds below. A few yards farther on, after you have reorganized yourself, you step into the deep cleft of Carlo Col. You are near your night's shelter. Turn left onto the Carlo Col Trail and follow it down a stony 0.25 mile. At the first sign of water the trail bears left to avoid it because it has taken over the old trail. From a little ridge you descend in a wide curve to the right and return to the streamlet. Continue straight across and up a steep bank to the Carlo Col Shelter. (The Carlo Col Trail descends on the left beside the water to Success Pond Road 2.5 miles away.) The Carlo Col Shelter is built of logs like the Gentian Pond Shelter.

Fourth Day: Carlo Col Shelter to Full Goose Shelter

Distance: 4½ miles

Walking time: 4 hours

This day's hike features Goose Eye Mountain and barren ridges such as you might see in Labrador. It begins with a starting climb from Carlo Col Shelter back to the Mahoosuc Trail. You'll feel the morning coolness because the shelter's elevation is 3000 feet. Turn left from the Carlo Col Trail onto the Mahoosuc Trail. Mount Carlo, elevation 3565, rises ahead, and the trail leads up through spruces. But the climb warms you before you emerge on Mount Carlo's bare summit, perhaps hidden in morning mist. You've been climbing 45 minutes if you start your day sensibly, without straining, so clearing skies and valleys may reveal the northern panorama of Success Pond and the mountains you saw yesterday afternoon before Carlo Col.

Beyond the summit, the trail crosses a bog on split log walkways, descends into spruce woods, then goes up a ledge and down again, often through more black mud or above it on walkways. You come out onto a barren slope, which if horizontal and near the Arctic Circle could be called tundra. Your eyes are at once attracted to Goose Eye Mountain—ahead across a deep col—a distant pinnacle of rock.

Legend gives this mountain the early name of "Goose High," because the summit was an obstacle to migrating geese. The geese had to clear by a few wingbeats a rocky 3870-foot mass.

The descent from the barrens into evergreens becomes so steep and rough that you grab at spruces to help you swing down. Don't forget to test before entrusting serious weight and balance to a tree. As you approach the transition to the col, you may find water trickling across the trail from a spring on the left. The walk across the col beside wide patches of sphagnum moss near the spruces will take you only 5 minutes. Then Goose Eye Mountain!

You can test your leg muscles on the stone steps, which offer steady climbing. The steepness eases at a swing left, then up you go again. Goose Eye Mountain shows you how to climb (with the aid of AT trail crew work) 500 feet in 0.25 mile.

There are more walkways, leading to more stone steps, which bear right to avoid a chimney in the mountainside. At the upper end of the stone steps, carefully climb to the log stairs. You emerge on a less demanding section, which takes you to open views over low scrub and ledges. Ahead, Goose Eye's pinnacle appears clearly. There's a last scramble in the scrub and you top out on the east shoulder of the mountain at treeline.

The Mahoosuc Trail turns sharp right. Branching left, the Goose Eye Trail leads over the summit rocks. (And down to the Success Pond Road.) You'll want to dump your pack at the junction and climb the 200 yards to Goose Eye's peak for a rest, a snack, and the views.

Return to your pack and continue east on the Mahoosuc Trail. You walk along a rocky ridge, bare except for scattered small spruces, and you can see your next climb—East Peak. But first you traverse a section of evergreens to a col, then ascend to the bare summit. On it there's a left turn, north, down from East Peak. Watch for cairns. The trail descends across a great sloping barrens, toward the eastern corner of spruces. The seemingly subarctic flora and shrubs along the trail are so low you look off to your next destination, North Peak, and in the distance to northern forests and lakes.

You enter the scrub you've been approaching. The trail drops to the col before North Peak. The woods open up among larger spruces. At a damp, wooded ravine, you come upon small pools of water cupped in sphagnum moss.

North Peak is steep, too. The wide barrens resemble treeline areas in the Presidentials and Franconias, although here vegetation extends to the highest ground. Much of the rock is crumbly and soft. Gravel in the trail crunches under your boots.

Clouds and rain often settle over the range, and winds are icy. If you must brave a drenching exposure on a ridge such as Goose Eye's North Peak, you face subarctic winds and temperatures.

From North Peak, the Mahoosuc Trail continues east along open ground beyond the summit. You follow and descend through scrub and barrens into head-high spruces. You find yourself walking down over ledges among older trees. Another mountain looms before you. The trail seems to vanish, however, at a wall of brush, and you are hemmed in by a small ledge on your right.

Face the ledge and pull yourself up. You emerge by Full Goose Shelter where you'll spend the night. It opens toward Fulling Mill Mountain and the precipitous valleys of Bull Branch and Goose Eye Brook. Beyond are the mountains that rise above and conceal Grafton Notch.

This shelter for 10 hikers is built of boards and sawn timbers. To get a drink of water, walk past the front and take the steep path down to the spring.

Fifth Day: Full Goose Shelter to Speck Pond Shelter

Distance: 5 miles

Walking time: 7 hours

The Mahoosuc Trail continues north from Full Goose Shelter by dropping down the overlook in front of the shelter, to a ravine that is only an infinitesimal hint of the Mahoosuc Notch to come. But first, the south peak of Fulling Mill Mountain. You climb up a steady grade through evergreens and reach a meadow between two wooded summits. The trail turns left and you rapidly descend, in trees again, 1000 feet to the western end of Mahoosuc Notch. (At a junction, left, the Notch Trail comes in from the Success Pond Road.)

You turn sharply right and follow the Mahoosuc Trail down a pleasant slope among spruces at 2500 feet elevation. You are entering Mahoosuc Notch. The gentle approach leaves you unprepared for the gigantic rock slabs and chunks, which seem to have fallen from the high cliffs on either side. But they have not fallen recently; they are draped with moss and crusted with lichens.

The moss forms treacherous pads over crevices and caves. Be careful not to step on any moss that reaches from slab to slab. As you crawl under overhanging rocks, you hear water trickling deep down in caves. Winter chill comes to you from the ice caverns. You follow white paint marks as the trail twists and turns for 1 mile among the rocks. You should plan on at least 2 hours during which you'll be busy reaching for handholds, stepping wide, balancing, and creeping.

At the notch's eastern end, you resume normal woods hiking. The trail follows the brook past the site of a former small beaver pond. Below this, after entering big hardwoods, you turn left away from the brook, climb up a short distance, and bear right onto an old logging road. In a slabbing ascent, the trail rounds Mahoosuc Mountain.

The trail follows a logging road toward a sag known as Notch 2, until you cross a brook. After a rough section, you begin the day's second real climb as the trail swings up Mahoosuc Arm. Much of the way, the trail rises among tall, old spruces. Mahoosuc Arm extends 1200 feet above Mahoosuc Notch. About halfway, or 0.75 mile from the notch, you come to a seasonal brook in a rock sluice; don't count on water.

Climbing on, you enter evergreen scrub and begin to ascend sloping ledges. The trail follows cairns along rock worn by glaciers and ages of weathering. You come out on the bare ridge itself, Mahoosuc Arm, which is really a mountain almost 3800 feet high.

A big cairn and post on the open ledges mark the summit of Mahoosuc Arm. Here the Mahoosuc Trail turns right. (A cutoff trail to Speck Pond Trail forks left.) The Mahoosuc Trail jogs approximately south and then

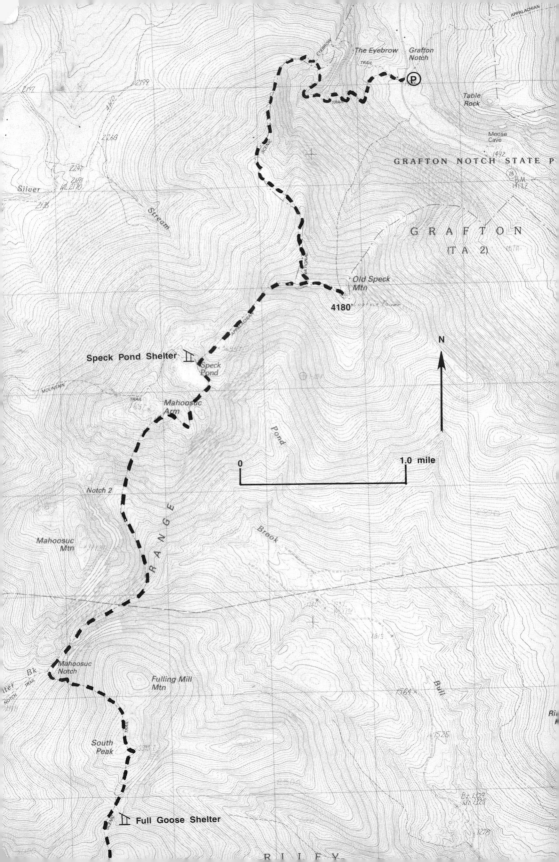

The Eyebrow
Grafton Notch
EYEBROW TRAIL
P

Table Rock

Moose Cave

GRAFTON NOTCH STATE P
1492
BM
1411.2

GRAFTON
(TA 2)

Silver

Stream

Old Speck
Mtn
4180'

N

Speck Pond Shelter
Speck Pond
APPALACHIAN

Mahoosuc
Arm

MOUNTAIN
TRAIL

0   1.0 mile

Pond

Notch 2

R A N G E

Brook

Mahoosuc
Mtn

1564

Bull

Mahoosuc
Notch
NOTCH TRAIL
Bk

Fulling Mill
Mtn
1525

South
Peak

Full Goose Shelter

R I L E Y

On Goose Eye Mountain

north along the ridge and enters occasional scrub between open meadows. Now going down more steeply
through spruce woods, you descend
to 3500 feet and Speck Pond. The
trail circles to the east shore, and at
the upper end you come to Speck Pond
Campsite, which includes the shelter
for 12 hikers, tent sites, and caretaker.
There is a fee for overnight camping.
A small, deep, mountain lake, Speck
Pond is the highest in Maine, and has
been measured 50 feet to the bottom.
Beavers may raise the depth at times
with a dam in the outlet, which is Pond
Brook. The pond reflects the surrounding pointed spruces, or sometimes,
due to its elevation, lies smothered in
clouds. (The Speck Pond Trail leaves
from the shelter for the Success Pond
Road.)

Sixth Day

Allowed for bad weather or to spend
at Speck Pond.

**Seventh Day: Speck Pond Shelter to
Grafton Notch**

Distance: 4¾ miles

Walking time: 4½ hours

Your departure in the morning should
be adjusted to the weather. Foggy daylight and gloomy spruce woods have

been known to brighten in an hour, and too-eager hikers have arrived at Old Speck's summit to find it shrouded in clouds, and by then descending to Grafton Notch have missed the spectacular scenery spread out in all directions from the observation tower. Now that you have been conditioned by the Mahoosucs, you should be able to climb Old Speck and descend to Grafton Notch in 4.5 hours. So wait awhile for clear skies.

Take the Mahoosuc Trail from Speck Pond Campsite northeast. Directly, it climbs up a large knoll, drops down, and then up and around another ridge. In the next little valley, you pass a spring east of the trail. You begin to climb up Old Speck along ledges that lead you on upward at the apex of their angles, which drop off on either side.

This rocky shoulder joins spruce woods, and the trail, bearing right, leads into them. The trail parallels for a time the blue paint blazes identifying the boundary of Grafton Notch State Park. You are nearing the highest elevation of your backpack week—4180 feet. As you approach the summit of Old Speck, you pass on your left the Old Speck Trail to Grafton Notch and the highway, ME 26. This trail will be the route of your descent. From this junction to the summit, a little over 0.25 mile, you may as well carry your pack along the more level section to the clearing in the evergreens surrounding the observation tower.

The view northward from the tower is toward Umbagog Lake and the Rangeley Lakes, whose waters shine like mirrors on a sunny day. To the southwest, the peaks, ravines, and barren heaths of the rugged range you've climbed over stretch away to the Presidentials.

From the summit clearing, retrace your steps along the Mahoosuc Trail to the Old Speck Trail. Turn right onto the Old Speck Trail for your 3.5-mile downward loop to the depths of Grafton Notch. First the trail takes you steeply down to a long northern ridge. As you begin this, the trail turns northwest where the Link Trail enters on your right. (The Link Trail gives steep access to the site of the former cabin for the fire warden near a small brook, about 0.25 mile. At the site, a trail from the summit's East Spur joins with the Link Trail.)

Walk past the Link Trail along the northern ridge for about 0.5 mile, with steady, sometimes rough, loss of altitude in the spruce/fir forest. The trail swings eastward among tall spruces and leaves the ridge at an outlook into the notch and down the Bear River valley to Newry, and nearby across the notch, to Baldpate Mountain. The Eyebrow Trail comes in on your left. (The Eyebrow Trail traverses the upper edge of an 800-foot cliff called The Eyebrow, and is not for backpackers.) Climb down to the right of the Eyebrow Trail junction on the Old Speck Trail. Stone steps, waterbars, and log steps will assist you for the remaining mile of this section, which has almost literally been attached to the mountainside by trail crews.

You cross a small stream, the head of Cascade Brook. The trail turns left and follows the south edge of the rock that carries the cascades. Then a right turn puts you on more log steps leading down into yellow birches and beeches. These deciduous trees indicate you've come down to a milder climate. The trail follows a series of switchbacks.

Grafton Notch is so narrow that you have scarcely 100 yards—after you pass the lower Eyebrow Trail entering on your left—of level walking till you reach the bulletin board and outline trail map, and step out onto the large parking area for the Grafton Notch State Park. (From the bulletin board, the AT continues east across ME 26 to climb over Baldpate Mountain on its way to Katahdin.)

Now you are back in the world of wheeled transportation for the first time in a week.

There is a major flaw in my character, to wit: I take serious subjects lightly, and light subjects seriously. Brooks are considered ordinarily nothing but light subjects. They are suitable for light lyrical verse, for instance. They have been a serious part of my life.

Thus too with the love of Nature. The subject of Nature only becomes serious when it is subjected to scientific inquiry.

Thus also with taking care of Nature or, to use its real meaning, taking care of our world.

This serious subject I take lightly. I suggest that the infrastructure of environmentalism—how I like this modern jargon!—is very simple. The basis for looking after our planet is birth control. Margaret Sanger laid out the solution years ago. Earth Day celebrants should place statues of her in every park and parade in her memory.

—Daniel Doan
"Notes"

Index

Let Backcountry Guides Take You There

Our experienced backcountry authors will lead you to the finest trails, parks, and back roads in the following areas:

50 Hikes Series

50 Hikes in the Maine Mountains
50 Hikes in Southern and Coastal Maine
50 Hikes in Vermont
50 Hikes in the White Mountains
50 More Hikes in New Hampshire
50 Hikes in Connecticut
50 Hikes in Massachusetts
50 Hikes in the Hudson Valley
50 Hikes in the Adirondacks
50 Hikes in Central New York
50 Hikes in Western New York
50 Hikes in New Jersey
50 Hikes in Eastern Pennsylvania
50 Hikes in Central Pennsylvania
50 Hikes in Western Pennsylvania
50 Hikes in the Mountains of North Carolina
50 Hikes in Northern Virginia
50 Hikes in Ohio
50 Hikes in Michigan

Walks and Rambles Series

Walks and Rambles on Cape Cod and the
    Islands
Walks and Rambles in Rhode Island
More Walks and Rambles in Rhode Island
Walks and Rambles on the Delmarva Peninsula
Walks and Rambles in Southwestern Ohio
Walks and Rambles in Ohio's Western Reserve
Walks and Rambles in the Western Hudson
    Valley
Walks and Rambles on Long Island
Walks and Rambles in and around St. Louis

25 Bicycle Tours Series

25 Bicycle Tours in Maine
30 Bicycle Tours in New Hampshire
25 Bicycle Tours in Vermont
25 Mountain Bike Tours in Vermont
25 Bicycle Tours on Cape Cod and the Islands
25 Mountain Bike Tours in Massachusetts
30 Bicycle Tours in New Jersey
25 Bicycle Tours in the Adirondacks
25 Mountain Bike Tours in the Adirondacks
30 Bicycle Tours in the Finger Lakes Region
25 Bicycle Tours in the Hudson Valley
25 Bicycle Tours in the Twin Cities and South-
    eastern Minnesota
30 Bicycle Tours in Wisconsin
25 Mountain Bike Tours in the Hudson Valley
25 Bicycle Tours in Ohio's Western Reserve
25 Bicycle Tours in Maryland
25 Bicycle Tours on Delmarva
25 Bicycle Tours in and around
    Washington, D.C.
25 Bicycle Tours in Coastal Georgia and the
    Carolina Low Country
25 Bicycle Tours in the Texas Hill Country
    and West Texas
The Mountain Biker's Guide to Ski Resorts

We offer many more books on hiking, fly-fishing, travel, nature, and other subjects. Our books are available at bookstores and outdoor stores everywhere. For more information or a free catalog, please call 1-800-245-4151 or write to us at The Countryman Press, PO Box 748, Woodstock, Vermont 05091. You can find us on the Web at www.countrymanpress.com.